9-1 GCS STUDY WILLIAM SHAKESPEARE'S *MACBETH* - Revision guide

by RJ Forster

ISBN-13:
978-1983493065

ISBN-10:
1983493066

CONTENTS

9-1 GCSE KEY STUDY NOTES – Macbeth

Brief Introduction

This book is aimed at GCSE students of English Literature who are studying William Shakespeare's *Macbeth*. The focus is on what examiners are looking for, especially since the changes to the curriculum in 2015, and here you will find each scene covered in detail. I hope this will help you and be a valuable tool in your studies and revision.

Criteria for high marks

Make sure you use appropriate critical language (see glossary of literary terms at the back). You need your argument to be fluent, well-structured and coherent. Stay focused!

Analyse and explore the use of form, structure and the language. Explore how these aspects affect the meaning. Make connections between texts and look at different interpretations. Explore their strengths and weaknesses. Don't forget to use supporting references to strengthen your argument.

Analyse and explore the context.

Best essay practice

There are so many way to write an essay. Although exam boards discourage formulas, many schools use **PEE** for paragraphs: point/evidence/explain. Others use **PETER**: point/evidence/technique/explain/reader; **PEEL**: point, example, explain, link; **PEEE**: point/evidence/explain/explore. Whichever method you use, make sure you mention the **writer's effects**. This generally is what most students forget to add. You must think of what the writer is trying to achieve by using a particular technique and what is actually achieved. Do not just spot techniques and note them. You may get some credit for using appropriate technology, but unless you can comment on the effect created on the reader and/or the writer's intention, you will miss out on most of the marks available.

Essay planning

In order to write a good essay it is necessary to plan. In fact, it is best to quite formulaic in an exam situation, as you won't have much time to get started. Therefore I will ask you to learn the following acronym: **DATMC (Definition, Application, Terminology, Main, Conclusion**. Some schools call it: **GSLMC (General, Specific, Link, Main, Conclusion)**, but it amounts to the same thing. The first three letters concern the introduction. (Of course, the alternative is to leave some blank lines and write your introduction after you have completed the main body of your essay, but it is probably not advisable for most students).

Let us first look at the following exam question, which is on poetry (of course, the same essay-planning principles apply to essays on novels and plays as well).

QUESTION: Explore how the poet conveys **feelings** in the poem.

STEP ONE: Identify the **keyword** in the question. (I have already done this, by highlighting it in **bold**). If you are following GSLMC, you now need to make a **general statement** about what feelings are. Alternatively, if you're following DATMC, simply **define** 'feelings'. For example, 'Feelings are emotion states or reactions or vague, irrationals ideas and beliefs'.

STEP TWO: If you are following GSLMC, you now need to make a **specific statement** linking feelings (or whatever else you've defined) to how they appear in the poem. Alternatively, if you're following DATMC, simply define which 'feelings' **apply** in this poem. For example, 'The feelings love, fear and guilt appear in this poem, and are expressed by the speaker in varying degrees.'

STEP THREE: If you are following GSLMC, you now need to make a **link statement** identifying the methods used to convey the feelings (or whatever else you've defined) in the poem. Alternatively, if you're following DATMC, simply define which **techniques** are used to convey 'feelings' in this poem. For example, 'The poet primarily uses alliteration to emphasise his heightened emotional state, while hyperbole and enjambment also help to convey the sense that the speaker is descending into a state of madness.

STEP FOUR: Whether you are following GSLMC or DATMC, the next stage is more or less the same. The main part of the essay involves writing around **six paragraphs**, using whichever variation of PEEE you prefer. In my example, I will use **Point, Evidence, Exploration, Effect** on the listener. To make your essay even stronger, try to use your quotations chronologically. It will be easier for the examiner to follow, which means you are more likely to achieve a higher grade. To be more specific, I recommend that you take and analyse two quotations from the beginning of the poem, two from the middle, and two at the end.

STEP FIVE: Using Carol Ann Duffy's poem, 'Stealing', here's an example of how you could word one of your six paragraphs: **(POINT)** 'Near the beginning of the poem, the speaker's determination is expressed.' **(EVIDENCE)** 'This is achieved through the words: 'Better off dead than giving in'. **(EXPLORATION).** The use of 'dead' emphasizes how far the speaker is prepared to go in pursuit of what he wants, although there is a sense that he is exaggerating (hyperbole). **(EFFECT)** The listener senses that the speaker may be immature given how prone he is to exaggerate his own bravery.

STEP SIX: After writing five or more paragraphs like the one above, it will be time to write a **conclusion**. In order to do that, it is necessary to sum up your previous points and evaluate them. This is not the time to introduce additional quotations. Here is an example of what I mean: 'To conclude, the poet clearly conveys the speaker's anger. Although the listener will be reluctant to completely sympathise with a thief, there is a sense that the speaker is suffering mentally, which makes him an interesting and partially a sympathetic character. By using a dramatic monologue form, the poet effectively conveys the speaker's mental anguish, which makes it easier to more deeply understand what first appears to be inexplicable acts of violence.

Other tips
Make your studies active!

Don't just sit there reading! Never forget to annotate, annotate and annotate!

Macbeth
AQA (New specification starting in 2015)
If you're studying for an AQA qualification in English Literature, there's a good chance your teachers will choose this text to study. There are good reasons for that: it's moralistic and familiar to students. The text encourages us to think about right and wrong.
However, one of the difficulties is the language. That can't be helped, bearing in mind that part A of the exam paper involves answering questions on Shakespeare, whereas part B is all about the 19th-century novel.
To further complicate things, the education system is in a state of flux: that means we have to be ready for constant change. Of course, everyone had got used to grades A,B and C meaning a pass. It was simple, it was straightforward and nearly everyone understood it. Please be prepared that from this day henceforward, the top grade will now be known as 9. Grade 4 will be the equivalent of a C grade, although the government want students to aim for a good pass, or a low B, which will be grade 5.
Now onto the exam itself. As I said, Paper 1 consists of Shakespeare and the 19th-century novel. It is a written closed book exam (in other words you are not allowed to have the texts with you), which lasts one hour 45 minutes. You can score 64 marks, which amounts to 40% of your GCSE grade. The other 60% is gained from paper 2, which is all about modern texts, poetry and unseen poetry. But enough about paper 2, as our concern here is paper 1 and more specifically section A: Shakespeare.

In section B, students will be expected to write in detail about an extract from the novel they have studied in class and then write about the novel as a whole. Just for the record, the choices of novel are the following: *The Strange Case of Dr Jekyll and Mr Hyde* by Robert Louis Stevenson, *A Christmas Carol* and *Great Expectations* by Charles Dickens, *Jane Eyre* by Charlotte Brontë, *Frankenstein* by Mary Shelley, *Pride and Prejudice* by Jane Austin, and The Sign of Four by Sir Arthur Conan Doyle.

Another important thing to consider is the fact that for section B of Paper 1, you will not be assessed on assessment objective 4 (AO4), which involves spelling, punctuation, grammar and vocabulary. This will be assessed on section A of paper 1, which is about Shakespeare, and it will be worth 2.5% of your overall GCSE grade. In terms of raw marks, it is worth 4 out of 64. So for once, we need not concern ourselves with what is affectionately known as 'SPAG' too much.

However, it is necessary to use the correct literary terminology wherever possible to make sure we maximise our marks on assessment objective2 (AO2). AO2 tests how well we can analyse language form and structure. Additionally, we are expected to state the effect the writer tried to create and how it impacts on the reader. This brings me onto assessment objective 1 (AO1), which involves you writing a personal response to the text. It is important that you use quotations to backup your points of view. Like AO2, AO1 is worth 15% of your GCSE on Paper 1.

Assessment objective 3 (AO3) is worth half of that, but nevertheless it is important to comment on context to

make sure you get as much of the 7.5% up for grabs as you can.
So just to make myself clear, there are 30 marks available in section B for your answer on the 19th-century novel. Breaking it down even further, you will get 12 marks maximum the backing up your personal opinion with quotations, an additional 12 marks for analysing the writer's choice of words for effect (not forgetting to use appropriate terminology - more on that see the glossary at the back of this book), and six marks for discussing context.

As you can see, we've got a lot to get through so without further ado let's get on with the actual text itself and possible exam questions.

Previous exam questions
Notwithstanding the governmental changes to the grading system, it is still good practice to go over previous exam papers. I'm looking at a specimen paper, which asks students to read an extract from Act 1 Scene 5, which begins: 'The raven himself is hoarse'. It ends with: 'Hold, hold!'.
Students are expected to read the extract and comment about how Shakespeare presents Lady Macbeth as a powerful woman. Students should say how that is shown in the extract itself and also on the whole novel. Despite the changes to the syllabus which have made GCSEs more difficult to pass, future questions are likely to be very similar. Of course, it could be about a different

character, but it will involve looking at the extract for the first part of the question and then moving on to discuss the whole play. That's the format and is unlikely to change in the near future. So no worries there then!

To make sure that you meet AQA's learning objectives and get a high mark, make sure you go into the exam knowing something about the following:

- the plot
- the characters
- the theme
- selected quotations/details
- exam skills

Now, we will be going through each of those objectives in turn, so you should be well prepared for the exam itself.

Tragedy

According to Aristotle, tragic drama should include both pity and terror which would ultimately lead to **catharsis**. The purpose of tragedy would be best served by a person who is neither completely good nor completely bad morally. In terms of the plot, the ideal would be one whereby the protagonist suffers a reversal in fortune (**peripeteia**) which takes him or her from happiness to misery as a result of some tragic flaw or error (**hamartia**). Along the way, the protagonists should have some moments of insight (**anagnorisis**), when he or she can see exactly how things are.

Tragedy could be subversive even in Elizabethan times. Sir Philip Sidney, for example, said in 1595 that tragedies could 'maketh kings fear to be tyrants'.

Meanwhile, GWF Hegel (1770-1831) claims that tragedy shows what happens when a partial good collides with a partial evil. The audience feel pain watching the destruction of one of these sides or both, but it leads to 'the true ethical Idea '.

Influenced by Hegel, AC Bradley (1851-1935) claimed in 1904 that tragedy emerges from inner conflict and outer conflict. Looking at Macbeth, he wrote: 'treasonous ambition in Macbeth collides with loyalty and patriotism in Macduff and Malcolm: here is the outward conflict. These powers or principles equally collide in the soul of Macbeth himself: here is the inner. And either by itself could make the tragedy '. Bradley believes that the most deeply felt emotion by an audience watching the tragedy is 'the impression of waste '.

Jonathan Dollimore claims that Elizabethan and Jacobean tragedy could be effective in subverting contemporary gender stereotypes. He says the crisis of confidence in the church and state helped plays to do this.

Like *Richard II*, *Macbeth* questions the rights and privileges of kings and raises the possibility of treason. These were issues that King James I, who ascended the throne in 1603, was very concerned about. He had written *The True Law of Free Monarchies* (1598) about the supreme power of the king, but was aware of the dangers of tyranny, which is why he penned *Basilikon Doron* (1599).

Context

For *Macbeth*, Shakespeare mainly referred to Raphael Holinshed's *Chronicles of England, Scotlande, and Irelande*. Shakespeare used a lot of poetic licence with the character of Banquo, as he was thought to be an ancestor of James I. As not all chroniclers were flattering in their description of Banquo, Shakespeare decided to modify his character and not portray him as a rebel and assassin. In Holinshed, King Duncan is younger and weaker than he appears to be in Macbeth. Once Duncan is murdered, Macbeth rules for 10 years in the historical account. Shakespeare merged this account with the murder of King Duff, who was dispatched by Donwald. By setting the play in the 11th century, Shakespeare effectively sidestepped censorship, which had resulted in other topical plays being closed down. Treason was a very sensitive subject, especially after the Earl of Gowrie tried to kill King James I while he stayed with him in Perth, Scotland in 1600. Five years later, of course, the Gunpowder Plot, further alerted James I to the dangers of assassination. Henry Garnett, a famous Jesuit, was implicated in this plot. Garnett exercised his right to 'equivocate' when asked to explain himself. This involved misleading questioner by not giving clear answers. This way, Catholics could avoid telling the truth without lying. This was important as many had divided loyalties between England and Rome, the home of their Catholic faith. Garnett's equivocation is more than hinted at in *Macbeth's* porter scene.

Witchcraft was also a very topical subject. King James I was convinced he was the target of daemonic attacks, and he took part in the North Berwick witch trials in 1591. Later, James I composed a book entitled *Demonology* (1597).

Language

The witches speak in a highly stylised, ritualised manner: first they speak in turn and then they deliver a conclusion in unison. These **alliterative choric couplets** are significant in that they introduce **paradox** and **ambiguity** into the play. For instance, 'fair is foul and foul is fair '. The language throughout is ambiguous. For instance, when the captain describes Macdonwald as 'worthy to be a rebel ', what does that say about Duncan describing Macbeth as a 'worthy gentleman '?

The Tiger mentioned by one of the witches could have been a ship that sailed from the Isle of Wight on 5 December 1604 returning after 567 days at sea. That ship was also called *Tiger* and had endured a tempestuous voyage.

Meanwhile, the **unstable language** in the play mirrors the unstable political situation at the time of the first performances.

There is **dramatic irony** which is employed as a linguistic device when Duncan says of the previous Thane of Cawdor: 'he was a gentleman on whom I built/an absolute trust '. The irony is increased when Macbeth takes over the mantle of the Thane of Cawdor and also declares his loyalty.

Note that at the time the Scottish Crown did not necessarily the get passed on to the oldest son of the existing monarch. Macbeth shows his irritation with tight **rhyming couplets** after the revelation that Malcolm will succeed Duncan as King.

Critics

Terry Eagleton says that the witches 'scorn male power ' by wearing beards. This can be considered positive subversion of is the social hierarchy.

Meanwhile, the critics AC Bradley and G Wilson Knight could be accused of reductionism, as they see much of Macbeth as good versus evil. Similarly, seeing the play as just the conflict between order and disorder may also be too simplistic.

Genre

Like later Gothic novels, the play has a number of doubles, but in the verbal sense as opposed to characterisation. For instance, the captain says 'as cannons overcharged with double cracks,/so they doubly redoubled strokes upon the foe '. This is reminiscent of the witches chant 'double, double, toil and trouble'. When it comes to gender, Macbeth is not misogynistic describing his wife as 'my dearest partner of greatness '. Lady Macbeth refers to him in more female terms suggesting he is 'to fall of the milk of human kindness '. K. Ryan suggests that this phrase indicates a 'tender nurturing attention to others'. Traditional ideas of both masculinity and femininity are transgressed in the play, particularly by Lady Macbeth who wants to exchange her milk for gall.

Using the semantic field of theology, law and ethics as well as fishing, riding and jumping metaphors Macbeth effectively conveys his intellectual and emotional instability.

Interestingly, Seaton is around as Macbeth and Lady Macbeth come close to their demise. It is almost as if they are descending into hell. This hell was being referred to by the porter, who some consider to be a parody of St Peter. He abandons the place because it's too cold.

Context in bullet points

I've tried to filter out the relevant historical events and only have included those that may have influenced Shakespeare or his play, *Macbeth*.

England in 1606

At that time, many believed:

- geocentricism rather than heliocentricism: the sun went round the earth, despite Copernicus's idea that the opposite is the case being proven by Galileo later in 1610

- everything was ordered by God - the monarchy and the church were founded by God

Government
- Essex is executed for treason (like Macbeth, some people consider him too ambitious)
- Queen Elizabeth I died in 1603 and was succeeded by King James I, who was also King James VI of Scotland.
- The succession of King James I to the throne united both kingdoms.
- The union of the crowns was unpopular with many Scots and many English
- In 1603, a law was passed illegalising conjuring up evil spirits and/or grave-robbing
- the Puritans and Catholics arguing in Scotland
- the Gunpowder Plot 1605, an unsuccessful attempt to blow up the Houses of Parliament

Religion
- all children were baptised into the Church of England
- absences from divine services at church could be punishable by fines
- church records kept tabs on the population
- the authorities were alerted to anyone following unusual religious practices, who could be politically dangerous
- approved teaching of religion was received through 'homilies' in parish churches
- the Book of Common prayer was in every church
- the Bible was read aloud in English

Language

- there was very little English literature at the start of the 16th century
- Latin was the language of international scholarship
- translations from Latin resulted in more English words being made and its grammar becoming more flexible
- by the end of the 16th century, English as a language was much more well-developed. Now it was ready for wordplay, especially puns

Drama

- Elizabethans read and translated Roman plays
- all-male acting companies travelled from town to town, setting up in open places or in halls (continuing until the 17th century outside of London)
- In 1576, the Theatre, the first purpose-built playhouse was erected in London
- most of Shakespeare's plays were performed in the Globe
- playhouses were closed in the summer to prevent the spread of diseases, like the plague
- there was censorship of plays, but its severity varied

11th-century Scotland

- families and clans were at war
- each side was led by a thane, and his castle was an important powerbase
- murder and revenge were rife
- the government included the King and a council made up of warlords and church leaders

- communication was difficult because of the
  landscape

The 'real' Macbeth

- born around 1005
- his family ruled Moray and Ross
- his father was murdered by his cousins
- he descended from Malcolm the second
  (Macbeth's grandfather)
- she married Gruach (granddaughter to a high
  King of Scotland)
- he became Mormaer (great steward) of Moray
- overthrew King Duncan of Strathclyde around
  1040. Macbeth thought he had the right to become
  king through the rules of tanistry (which involved
  the throne being passed down the mother's line:
  for instance, the heir or 'tanist' could be the son of
  the reigning king's sister, instead of the oldest son
  of the king. Tanistry was later replaced by
  primogeniture, but in the play, Malcolm's
  succession is neither tanistry nor primogeniture)

Macbeth - simplified plot with commentary

Act 1 Scene 1

The first witch simply asks when they should meet up
once more. Interestingly, she makes it clear that there are
only three choices, all involving inclement weather: in
thunder, lightning, or in rain.

The second witch replies that the next meeting will take
place after the battle is over and the noise of it has
subsided.

The third witch adds that the battle will be over before
sunset.

The first witch wants to know where the next meeting
will take place. The second witch replies that it should be

upon the heath. Once again, the third witch adds extra information, saying that Macbeth will arrive there too. After that, spirits call the witches. The first witch is called by Graymalkin, her cat, which is her familiar (or in other words, her special spirit in the shape of an animal). The second witch is called by Paddock. This has nothing to do with horseracing! Instead, it is a familiar in the shape of a toad. We don't find out the nature of the third witch's familiar. However, she tells it that she is on the way by saying: 'Anon.'

Before they fly away into the mist, the witches chant in unison: 'Fair is foul, and foul is fair / Hover through the fog and filthy air.'

Act 2 Scene 2

This scene is commonly known as the captain's scene. The captain is sometimes known as, or referred to as, a sergeant; but whatever his rank, he is more often than not portrayed as a valiant soldier. Indeed, it is difficult to foresee the captain being played in any other way. The captain is described by Duncan, the King of Scotland, and Malcolm, the king's son, as 'bloody' and 'hardy' respectively.

Duncan begins by saying, that judging by the captain's appearance, he's certainly been in the wars. Duncan means it quite literally. Therefore, the captain is the right man to ask about the rebellion against the king.

Malcolm confirms description this by saying that the sergeant fought valiantly to save him falling into enemy hands. He directly addresses the soldier, who is on his last legs, or mortally wounded, in many productions. The captain then tells his story. He begins by saying that it was hard to tell who would win the battle, initially. He compares the two armies to two exhausted swimmers, struggling in the water and hanging onto each other. He adds that although Macdonwald was aided and abetted by soldiers from Ireland and the Hebrides, he was also strengthened by Lady Luck (an imaginary figure presiding over the world and its fortunes). Luck has played a big part. So much so that the captain describes Lady Luck as Macdonwald's prostitute. Macdonwald is so lucky that the captain believes that Lady Luck is metaphorically sleeping with the rebel. It doesn't sound like a loving relationship, as there is a suggestion in the word 'whore' that money has changed hands. Perhaps it is a reference to the mercenaries fighting on Macdonwald's side. It is almost as if Macdonwald has to buy luck as well as mercenaries to fight his corner. Hence, Shakespeare has cleverly manipulated words to make us believe, through the captain's speech, that Macdonwald is tainted by money. Already, the audience will feel that Macdonwald is an unworthy character, who has to buy his victories, friends and lovers. The captain goes on to say that Macbeth was so brave that he laughed in the face of all danger and the misfortune coming his way, and cut a swathe through the ranks all the way to Macdonwald. Once he reached the rebel, Macbeth sliced him from his belly button to his mouth. Finally, he beheaded him and impaled Macdonwald's head upon the stake on top of the castle.

Duncan's response is to say how brave Macbeth is, which is understandable as the threat posed by Macdonwald has now been assigned to history. As well as that, Macdonwald's head impaled upon a stick on the castle walls will serve as a reminder to those that rebel against the king.

The captain then tells Duncan and Malcolm that his story is not quite over. He compares what happened next to a violent storm coming at the beginning of springtime. Likewise, the Norwegian king mounted a fresh attack upon the captain and his troops.

To this, Duncan asked the question as to whether or not Macbeth and Banquo were frightened by this new onslaught.

The captain's reply was that this new challenge was insignificant to them. To Macbeth and Banquo, they were about as scared as eagles would be if attacked by sparrows, or as a lion would be if attacked by rabbits. Let's not forget that eagles are often compared to kings as they are thought to be the most majestic birds. The same goes for lions, which are kings of the jungle and are also noted for their bravery. Once again, Shakespeare's use of language is a taste of what is to come. In other words, the mention of eagles and a lion foreshadow the plot, which see a new king take the throne.

The captain continues by saying that they fought twice as hard against the Norwegians, and he likens this to cannons firing twice as many cannonballs as they would normally. He suggests that Macbeth and Banquo wanted to bathe in their enemies' blood. The captain also suggests that the carnage was as horrific as Christ's crucifixion at Golgotha. At this point, the captain feels faint and asks for medical attention.

Duncan seems impressed with the captain. The king tells his attendants to take the captain somewhere where he can get medical help, but before that he compares the captain's words to his wounds. It's almost a half pun. Like his words, the captain's wounds bestow honour upon him.

As a captain leaves, Ross (who is portrayed as a war journalist in at least one version of the play) and Angus into the scene.

Duncan appears not to recognise them as he asks his son who it is. Malcolm replies that it is the Thane of Ross, a Scottish nobleman. Interestingly, Malcolm doesn't mention Angus, who has nothing to do with the special beef you can get in McDonald's!

Lennox is the next one to speak and he says that Ross's eyes give him away. He looks stressed. He looks like he has a story to tell.

Ross begins very respectfully by saying: 'God save the King'. Of course, it appears that it is Banquo and Macbeth who have saved King rather than God. Let's not forget Lady Luck was not on the king's side in this battle, according to the captain.

Duncan asks Ross where he's come from. To this, Ross replies he's come from Fife. It seems as if Fife is under the control of Norway, judging by the Norwegian flag flying from a mast that dominates the skyline. He mentions that the Norwegian king had put together an enormous army and was assisted by the disloyal Thane of Cawdor. Macbeth opposed these overwhelming forces, and is described as Bellona's bridegroom. In mythological terms, Bellona is the belligerent wife of Mars, the Roman god of war. It is interesting that Ross compares Macbeth to a woman's husband. Why not simply say that Macbeth was like Mars? It seems to be deliberate on the part of Shakespeare. It may suggest that Macbeth is unduly influenced by his female partner, as we shall see later. Ross continues by saying that Macbeth was finally victorious when he broke the enemy's fighting spirit.

Duncan declares how happy he is at this news, to which Ross replies that Sweno, the Norwegian king, now hopes to agree a peace treaty. However, Ross says the Scots would not allow the Norwegians to bury their dead until the enemy had retreated to St Colme's Inch and paid the sum of $10,000.

To this, Duncan replies that the disloyal Thane of Cawdor will never betray him again. He tells Ross to go and announce that the Thane of Cawdor will be executed. The Thane's titles will be taken away from him and given to Macbeth.

Ross says he'll get it done immediately and the scene ends with Duncan saying that the Thane of Cawdor's loss is Macbeth's gain. Of course, this statement is heavy with irony, as Macbeth will become a traitor just like his predecessor as Thane of Cawdor.

Act 1 Scene 3

The three witches appear and it begins with the first witch asking where the second witch has been. The second witch replies she's been killing pigs. The third witch asks the first witch what she's been doing. Prepare yourself for a long answer!

The first witch tells a story of a sailor's over-fed wife, who had chestnuts in her lap. The first witch asked the sailor's wife for one of the chestnuts, but the greedy woman told her to go away. Unfortunately for the food-loving wife, the witch knew where her husband was sailing to. It turns out that the sailor is the master of a ship called the *Tiger*, bound for Aleppo in Syria. The witch threatens to sail to Aleppo in a sieve, which is a kitchen utensil made of perforated metal used the straining. Of course, with all its holes, it's impossible for a conventional sieve to be buoyant in water. The fact that the witch can sail in one demonstrates how powerful she is. When she arrives in Aleppo, she says she will become a tailless rat and perform malicious acts upon the unsuspecting sailor.

The second witch declares that she will offer some assistance to the first witch: providing the wind to help her sail to Aleppo. The first witch approves of this act of kindness. Not to be outdone, the third witch offers even more wind. You have to wonder whether a Shakespearean pun, or double meaning, is going on at this stage. Perhaps the bawdy bard had flatulent witches in mind for this part of the play.

After the third witch offers more wind, the first witch replies that she already has control of all the winds from every port. She promises she will drain the life out of the sailor. She will prevent him from sleeping for 81 weeks. Once again, you have to wonder what Shakespeare had in mind. Perhaps he was thinking that the first witch would transform herself into a flatulent prostitute in each port and keep the sailor awake every night. However, her magic has limitations: she cannot make his ship sink. Nonetheless, she can still conjure up stormy seas. Then, she asks the other witches to look at what she's got.

The second witch wants to see and she says: 'Show me.' The first witch explains that she is holding a helmsman's severed thumb. She adds that this helmsman was drowned while he was returning home.

Suddenly, a drum is heard offstage. The third witch announces Macbeth's arrival. Then all three of them dance in a magic circle, which is necessary for their spell to take effect. It is rather like winding up an old-fashioned clock. If you don't turn the key to wind it up, the clock will not function.

The witches chant in unison that they are weird or, in other words, are supernatural with the power to control fate. Of course, the Fates, or the Parcae in Roman legend, and the Moirae in Greek mythology, were also known as 'the three sisters'. They were so powerful that even the gods were scared of them.

Macbeth and Banquo enter. Echoing the words of the witches, Macbeth says: 'So foul and fair day I have not seen.' In other words, it is a typical day in Britain: the weather is disgusting one minute, pleasant the next. You might say Britain's weather is an oxymoron in itself, but that's another story!

Banquo asks Macbeth how far it is to Forres, which is on the Moray coast (which sounds a bit like the aforementioned Moirai!) of Scotland. Then he sees the witches and asks what they are. He adds that they look strange and are dressed strangely. He can't believe that they are even from the Earth. He asks if they're alive. He asks if he and Macbeth can ask them questions. He adds that they seem to understand, as each of them has put a finger on their lips, suggesting perhaps that he should remain silent. Banquo remarks that they look like women, but that they have beards. Therefore he's most confused. Macbeth takes over and insists that the witches speak, if they can. He asks them what kind of creatures they are. The first witch hails him and calls him Thane of Glamis. That's not so surprising, as that is his title. The second witch calls him Thane of Cawdor. That is slightly more surprising to Macbeth, as he has just defeated the Thane of Cawdor in battle. The third witch calls him the future king to add to his surprise.

Banquo notices Macbeth's reaction and he asks him why he looks so startled and afraid. Then Banquo speaks to the witches to find out whether or not they're illusions. He tells the witches that they've greeted his noble friend and made him speechless with promises of an unlikely but glorious future. He reminds them that they have not said anything to him, personally, yet. However, Banquo makes it clear that he would like to know his future as well. He tells the witches he's not afraid of them.

The first witch simply greets Banquo by saying: 'Hail.' The second witch does the same, as does the third witch. The first witch tells Banquo that he is not as good as Macbeth, yet he is better in some indescribable way. The second witch adds that Banquo is not as happy as Macbeth, yet in some ways he's much happier. The riddles continue as the third witch tells Banquo that his descendants will be kings, although he will not become a king himself. She ends by greeting Macbeth and Banquo once again by saying the word: 'Hail'. The first witch repeats the same greeting.

Macbeth stops the witches, as he fears they're about to leave. He tells them he wants to find out more. He already knows he's the Thane of Glamis, as he inherited the title from his father, Sinel. It can be no coincidence that his father is called Sinel, as it sounds remarkably like the word 'sinner'. It's almost as if Shakespeare is suggesting that Macbeth has bad blood. However, Macbeth is not curious about why he was hailed as the Thane of Glamis. He wants to know how the witches have come to the conclusion that he is also the Thane of Cawdor. Bearing in mind that the Thane of Cawdor is rich and powerful, it seems a tad unlikely or impossible that Macbeth can hold this title too. He wants to know from the witches where they found out about these strange things. It is doubly strange that he is finding out about his future in such a desolate place. He demands that they speak again.

But the witches vanish. Banquo remarks that the Earth has bubbles, and that these witches are similar apparitions. Nevertheless, he is curious as to where they've gone to.

Macbeth surmises that they've vanished into thin air. He wishes they'd stayed, presumably so he could find out more information.

Banquo is questioning his and Macbeth's sanity. He can't believe what they've just seen. He wonders if they've been eating magic mushrooms or some other kind of drugs that cause hallucinations.

Macbeth reminds his friend, Banquo, that his children will be kings. To which, Banquo replies that Macbeth will be a king himself. Macbeth adds that he will also be Thane of Cawdor if he heard right. Banquo says that's exactly what he heard from the witches. Now he wonders who else is approaching, as Ross and Angus enter the scene.

Ross tells Macbeth that the king was happy to hear about his military successes. He adds that his exploits pleased the king so much that he became speechless with pleasure. The king was pleasantly surprised to hear that Macbeth fought against Macdonwald and the King of Norway on the same day. Not only that, Macbeth had no fear of death. Finally, Ross tells him that numerous messages were delivered informing the king of Macbeth's bravery.

Angus adds that the king sent them to say thank you and to bring Macbeth and Banquo back to him.

Unfortunately, they are not in a position to pay them.

However, Ross suggests that they can expect reward from the king himself and, as a taster, he begins to call Macbeth, the Thane of Cawdor.

Banquo is particularly shocked. He wonders aloud whether or not the devil can tell the truth.

Even Macbeth is shocked. He asks why they are calling him that when the Thane of Cawdor is still alive.

Angus replies that the man who was the Thane of Cawdor has now been sentenced to death. He adds that he doesn't really know exactly what the former Thane of Cawdor did wrong, but whatever it was it was treasonous, and therefore he has been stripped of his title and is facing death.

Now it's time for one of those famous Shakespearean asides, when the main character reveals something of his true nature. Here, Macbeth talks to himself so only the audience can hear him. He admits the best part of the prediction is yet to come, although he is now pleased to be the Thane of Cawdor as well as the Thane of Glamis. After speaking discreetly to himself and the audience, he thanks Ross and Angus for their good news. He then speaks privately to Banquo asking him whether or not he is beginning to hope that his children will be kings, given that part of the prediction made by the witches is already come true.

Banquo tells Macbeth that if you trust witches, then you may indeed well be on your way to becoming king.

However, Banquo says it's strange. He fears it could be a part truth told by the agents of evil to tempt good people to their own destruction. Then Banquo speaks to Ross and Angus, telling them he would like to have a word with them.

This leaves Macbeth to talk to himself in the audience once again. Macbeth is pleased that the witches have already told him two things that have come true. He now thinks it could be inevitable that he will become king as well. He quickly thanks Ross and Angus before continuing to talk to himself. He wonders how such a good thing can be a bad thing, and how a bad thing can be a good thing. Now that his Thane of Cawdor, he is considering murdering King Duncan. To him, the image is horrid, yet he can't help but consider it. The very thought makes his hair stand on end and his heart pound inside his chest. His imagination is more frightening than reality right now. The thought of committing a murder has shook him. So much so that he hardly knows who he is. He's speculating wildly about the future, now he finds it impossible to do anything. Suddenly, the most important things are those that don't exist.

Banquo notices Macbeth's unease and remarks that he is 'rapt', or dazed.

Macbeth is still continuing to talk to himself and the audience. He suggests that if it is fated for him to be king, then perhaps he should just let fate take its course. Perhaps he doesn't have to do anything.

Banquo says to Ross and Angus that Macbeth is not accustomed to these new titles. Like clothes, perhaps they will fit better in time.

Macbeth is still talking to himself in the audience, saying that whatever happens is going to happen. It's a rhyming couplet which makes it seem quite final.

Banquo reminds Macbeth that they are waiting for him. To this, Macbeth says sorry, he was distracted. He tells them that he won't forget how kind they've been to him. Now they should go to the king.

Then Macbeth speaks secretly to Banquo, saying that they have to remember what happened today. After reflecting upon the events, they should talk about it. Banquo agrees. Macbeth says there is no point talking anymore until that moment, and urges all of them to head to the king. So off they go.

Act 1 Scene 4

The scene begins with the sound of trumpets. Feralding the entrance of King Duncan, Lennox, Malcolm Donalbain and their attendants.

Duncan is the first to speak. The king asks if the former Thane of Cawdor has been executed yet. He also asks if those in charge of the execution have returned.

To that, Malcolm replies that they haven't come back yet. However, an insider saw Cawdor die and that same insider said that Cawdor confessed before his execution. Cawdor, apparently, begged for forgiveness and was very honourable in death. He threw away his life as if it were worth almost nothing.

Duncan replies that it's impossible to tell what man is thinking, just by looking at his face. He absolutely trusted Cawdor completely.

Interestingly, Macbeth enters just after Duncan has talked about trust. Along with Macbeth, enter Banquo, Ross and Angus. As Macbeth has performed heroics on the battlefield, Duncan is very pleased to see him and addresses him as 'worthiest cousin'. He adds that he was feeling guilty for not having thanked Macbeth enough for saving his realm. He says Macbeth has done so much so quickly that it has been impossible to reward him just as quickly. He says if Macbeth deserved less, then perhaps the reward an offer would have matched the deed. Instead, Macbeth has done more than can ever be repaid. Macbeth replies that the opportunity to serve his king is reward in itself. He only wants his king to accept what his subjects give him. He explains that it's all about duty: like a son to a father, or servants of a master, so is he bound by duty to his king. He feels duty-bound to do everything he can to keep the king safe, which is ironic given what he plans to do later.

Duncan replies that Macbeth is most welcome. He adds that Macbeth's career will begin to grow in stature now. Then he speaks to Banquo, calling him 'noble'. Duncan says Banquo deserves as much as Macbeth and everyone should know that. Duncan tells Banquo he wants to give him a hug!

You can understand if Banquo was disappointed, but it is a measure of the man that he appears not to be. Perhaps Banquo is of a warmer nature the Macbeth. Being loved may be more important to him than furthering his career prospects. While Duncan is hugging him, Banquo says that 'the harvest' belongs to the king, if he should 'grow'. By this, he is referring to how Duncan said he would make Macbeth 'full of growing'. Banquo, clearly, was to grow too. But the fruits of his labours will be given to the king. There is no sign of selfishness in the character Banquo.

Duncan then says how happy he is. He's so happy he has tears in his eyes. He wants his sons, relatives, lords and everyone who knows him to know that he intends to make his eldest son, Malcolm, his successor. (The throne did not necessarily pass from father to son in 11th-century Scotland.) Duncan says his son will now gain the title: Prince of Cumberland. Duncan promises that accolades will shine like stars on everybody else who deserves them, before inviting himself to Macbeth's castle at Inverness. By staying there, Duncan will feel even more in debt to Macbeth, he says.

Macbeth replies that he is accustomed to the kind of physical activity that needs to be done in preparation for the king. Therefore he will race ahead and let his wife know the good news. He says he's going.

Duncan describes Macbeth as 'worthy'.

As Macbeth prepares to leave, he talks to himself and the audience in an aside. He says the Malcolm being the Prince of Cumberland is 'a step' which he must jump over. Even that, or he'll fall flat on his face, as Malcolm is now in the Macbeth's way. Macbeth doesn't want the stars to shine light on his dark and terrible desires. It seems as if his eyes are going to be shocked by what his hands do. Obviously, he's talking about murder in a roundabout way. At that point, Macbeth exits.

Blissfully unaware of all of this, Duncan is still talking to Banquo. He's mid-conversation. He agrees with Banquo, that Macbeth is brave. Duncan has heard so many people praising Macbeth that it must be true. Duncan urges everyone to follow Macbeth, who was gone on ahead to prepare for the royal visit. He adds Macbeth has no equal. The trumpets sound and they all exit.

Act 1 Scene 5

This is often referred to as Lady Macbeth's letter scene, and unsurprisingly it begins with her reading a letter from her husband, Macbeth. She reads aloud: 'The witches met me on the last day of the battle after my success and reliable sources tell me they have supernatural

knowledge. I tried to question them more but they
disappeared. I stood there in shock and next thing I knew
messengers from the King arrived calling me the Thane
of Cawdor. That was exactly the same title that the weird
sisters had called me. They also called me a future king. I
thought I should let you know about this, 'my dearest
partner of greatness', so you can celebrate too. Keep it
secret for now and see you soon.
At this point she looks up from the letter, and says: you
are the thane of Glamis and Cawdor and you will get
what's promised. But I'm afraid that you are too soft to be
an opportunist. You have ambition and you want to be
powerful, but you lack the nasty streak you need to be a
success. You want to do everything like a good holy man.
You don't want to cheat but you want things that are not
yours. You're afraid to do what you have to do to get
those things. So come home quickly, so I can persuade
you. The Fates appear to be on your side.
At this point a servant enters and lady Macbeth asks him
or her what's happening. The servant replies the King is
coming tonight.
Lady Macbeth says it's crazy! Macbeth is with the king
and wouldn't he have notified home in advance so she
could prepare?
Seven apologises but says it is the truth. Macbeth is on
the way and sent a messenger on ahead, who has already
arrived. That messenger is breathless and exhausted.
Lady Macbeth says take good care of the messenger as he
brings good news.
The servant leaves and Lady Macbeth continues her
soliloquy, saying the messenger is short of breath and
hoarse like a croaking 'raven'. (Blackbirds, of course,
foreshadow death, while the word 'croak' also signifies

the same thing.) She tries to conjure up the spirits to give her murderous thoughts and make a less like a woman more like a man. She wants to be full of cruelty. She wants her blood to thicken so she doesn't feel any remorse. She wants to feel less than human so she can carry out her plans. She asks the spirits to turn the milking her breasts into acid, and she wants the night to be full of thick smoke so she can carry out murder without the heavens seeing anything untoward.

Now Macbeth enters, and his wife calls him the great thane of Glamis and the worthy Thane of Cawdor. She says Sue who have a title greater than both of those. She adds his letter has taken into a future that feels already present.

Macbeth replies that Duncan is coming tonight. His wife wants to know when Duncan is leaving. To which, Macbeth replies that it will be tomorrow.

Lady Macbeth says Duncan will never see tomorrow. She adds that Macbeth's face is easy to read like a book. She advises him to look more welcoming to his king and more like an 'innocent flower'. Nevertheless, he can still be the snake that hides underneath the flower. She reminds him that the King must be looked after, so she says she'll take care of business for the sake of their joint futures.

Macbeth says they should talk about it more later. His wife replies that he should make himself look more relaxed. If Macbeth looks worried, it will arouse suspicion. She tells him to leave everything else to her. Then they exit.

Act 1 Scene 6

Music from an instrument, which sounds like an oboe, plays. The stage is lit by torches. Duncan enters with

Malcolm, Donalbain, Banquo, Lennox, Macduff, Ross, Angus and their attendants.

Duncan begins by saying that the castle is a pleasant place, with sweet and which appeals to his gentleness.

Banquo remarks that it is such a hospitable place that the house martins build their nests on the castle walls. He describes the air as 'delicate'.

Lady Macbeth enters and Duncan calls her 'honoured hostess', which indicates that he is expecting a high level of hospitality and certainly not murder. He says that the love he gets from his subjects can be inconvenient at times, but he still accepts it. Likewise, he's inconveniencing her by being at the castle.

She replies that even if they'd doubled the effort it wouldn't be enough compared to the honours that have been bestowed upon the Macbeth family. It's interesting she uses the word 'double', as earlier featured in the captain's speech about Macbeth's bloody battle and it also featured in the witches' magic spell. The word 'double' is frequently used in the study of Gothic literature, but it has a different meaning here. Lady Macbeth says she's welcoming the king and his entourage as guests.

Duncan asks where's the Thane of Cawdor. They tried to overtake him, and he rode so swiftly that he beat them to the castle. Interestingly, he describes Macbeth's love as 'sharp as his spur'. By the night's end, Duncan will feel exactly how sharp that love is.

Lady Macbeth tells Duncan she and husband are servants to the team and always at his disposal. As well is that, they are ready to give the king back everything that is his. Duncan asks for her hand, and tells her to bring him to his host, Macbeth. He says he loves him dearly and will continue to bestow honours upon him. They all exit.

Act 1 Scene 7

Like the last scene, hautboys (old-fashioned oboes) are playing and torches are lit.

Then Macbeth says if we're going to do it, then we should get it done quickly. If killing the king would solve all problems, catching them all in a type of fishnet, then he would putting his life and soul at risk just to do it. He reminds himself that there are punishments to consider. Violence breeds violence. Justice is distributed equally. We all have to drink from the poisoned chalice, or cup. (Interestingly, the England football manager's job is often described as the 'poisoned chalice', as it appears to be a cursed accolade.) He then mentions the two types of trust involved: 1) he is Duncan subject, so should protect him and 2) he is Duncan's host, so should close the door in the face of any murderous and not commit it himself! He adds that Duncan has been humble, incorruptible and therefore will be backed by the Angels of heaven who will sing out about the injustice of the killing. Macbeth also personifies Pity, saying it will ride like the wind to spread the awful news. However, that wind will be drowned by tears. Therefore, he has 'no spur' or motivation to make himself commit this act. All he has is his ambition, which jumps too high for 'intent', or the reason why he's doing this, and crashes down upon it. Then Lady Macbeth enters and Macbeth asks her if she has any news. She replies that Duncan has almost finished his dinner. Then she asks Macbeth why he left the dining room.

Macbeth asks her if Duncan has been asking for him. To which, she replies of course he has. Then Macbeth tells that they cannot continue with this plan. He reminds her that the king has honoured him and enhanced his popularity. Macbeth says he enjoys being popular, and he doesn't want throwaway this feeling so quickly.

Lady Macbeth is angry and replies that his 'hope' must've been 'drunk' before. She wonders if his hope 'has' gone to sleep and woken up a greener and paler colour. She says this is a watershed as far as their love is concerned. She questions his bravery. She asks him if he will take the crown that he wants, or whether he will live like a coward instead. She teases him for saying 'I can't' after saying 'I want to'. It reminds her of the proverbial cat who loves fish, but doesn't want to get his paws wet.

Macbeth pleads with her to be quiet. He says he will only dares to do when a proper man would do. If someone dared to do more, then he would not be a man. Lady Macbeth is incensed. She replies that if he wasn't a man then what was he when he first mentioned doing this? She says when he dared to do it then he was a man. If he goes one step further by doing what he thought about doing and he will be much more of a man. Before it wasn't the right time or the right place, but he had the guts to consider murder. Now the time and place the right he's having second thoughts. She adds that although she has enjoyed having a baby drinking her milk, she would have slashed its brains out if she had promised to do it, the way as Macbeth has sworn to kill Duncan.

Macbeth asks what will happen if they fail, but Lady Macbeth questions that. She says they can't fail if Macbeth is courageous. While Duncan is asleep, after his long trip to Inverness, she'll get his two servants so drunk that they won't remember anything. While there are asleep, she and Macbeth will be able to do anything to the unguarded Duncan. Whatever they do, all the blame will go on the drunken servants.

Macbeth seems delighted, saying that she should only give birth to male children, as she is so masculine and courageous. He adds that once they have covered the two servants with blood and use their daggers, people will surely believe they are the culprits, won't they?

Lady Macbeth replies that it will be difficult to imagine it happen any other way. Plus, she and Macbeth will make sure they're crying loudly when they find out the news that Duncan has died.

Macbeth tells his decided once and for all to go through with this. He says he will use every muscle in his body to make sure he can commit this awful crime. He tells to go about her business of being a friendly hostess and to hide her 'false heart' with a 'false face'. Then they both exit.

Act 2 Scene 1

Banquo enters with his son, Fleance, who is holding a torch.

Banquo asks his son how the night is going. His son replies that he hasn't heard the clock striking but the moon has disappeared. (Therefore, it appears to be very dark on stage.)

Banquo says the moon usually disappears at midnight. His son respectfully replies that it's probably later than midnight now.

Banquo tells his son to take his sword. He says the heavens are being mean with their light, judging by the darkness all around. He gives him something else too, possibly a shield, before saying he's tired yet he cannot sleep. He's been having nightmares.

Then Macbeth enters with a servant, who is also carrying a lighted torch (not to be confused with a modern-day torch with Duracell batteries!). Banquo hears someone coming and tells his son to give him back the sword. He shouts out 'Who's there?'

Macbeth replies: 'A friend.' Banquo asks him why he's not asleep yet. He reminds him the king's already in bed and in a very good mood to give out presents. He gives Macbeth a diamond which he says is from the king to Macbeth's wife for the incredible hospitality.

Macbeth modestly says anyone prepared for the Kings visit, so couldn't be quite as hospitable as they wanted to be.

Banquo says everything has been alright though. But then he mentions the dreamy had last night about the three witches. He reminds Macbeth that they told him some truth about the future.

Macbeth says he doesn't think about the witches anymore. But he says when they have an hour to spare, they can talk about it again if he wants to.

Banquo says whenever you're ready we can talk about it. Macbeth tells Banquo that if he stays loyal to him, he will benefit when the time is right.

Banquo says he'll consider it as long as he can keep a clear conscience.

Macbeth tells him to relax for now, and Banquo says the same to you.

At this point, Banquo and Fleance leave. Macbeth now speaks to his servant, telling him to go and tell Lady Macbeth to ring the bell when his drink is ready. Then he tells him to go to bed. The servant duly exists.

Then Macbeth makes one of his most famous speeches, which begins: 'Is this a dagger I see before me'. In some productions, you can actually see a knife or the image of a knife in front of Macbeth, whereas in others he is simply grasping at thin air. He speaks to the dagger, real or imaginary, saying he wants to hold it. Then he says he can't touch it but he can still see it. Then he wonders if he is hallucinating. Then he compares the imaginary dagger with a physical one he takes out. He then tells the dagger and its leading him somewhere where he was going already and that he was planning to use a weapon just like this. He says his eyesight must be the one sense it's not working very well. Either that, or it's the only one that's working properly. He says he can still see the imaginary dagger, with blood stains on. Then he says to himself that there is no dagger there. He says murder is making him see one. He says half the world is asleep, enduring nightmares. Meanwhile, which are offering sacrifices to their goddess, Hecate (pronounced HEkit, or HEkaTEE; goddess of the moon and sorcery). He then personifies murder, describing it as being woken up by the howls of the wolf. He continues to describe murder as a person, with it moving as quietly as Tarquin, the last king of Rome who infamously raped Lucretia thus ending the dynasty.

Macbeth then speaks to the ground, telling you not to listen to the direction he's walking in. He tells the ground not to echo back and break the silence, which is more appropriate to what he's about to do. He realises that Duncan is living all the while he is talking, and that the more he talks the less courageous he feels. Therefore, he decides to go. He says the murder is then as good as done. He can hear the bell, inviting him to do it. He tells Duncan not to hear the bell, because for the king it is a death knell summoning him to heaven or hell.

Act 2 Scene 2
Lady Macbeth enters saying that the alcohol that the servants drank has also made her courageous. (Dutch

courage, we might call that!) Then she listens carefully. She hears an owl shrieking, and a man ringing the bell. She assumes that Macbeth is now killing the King. The doors to Duncan's bedroom are open, and the drunken servants are making a mockery of their jobs by snoring, when they should be protecting the king. They are so drunk and drugged, that it is almost impossible to tell whether the servants or alive or dead.

Then, off stage, Macbeth calls out, wondering who is there. Lady Macbeth doesn't see him or recognise his voice so she says to herself that she's afraid the servants woke up and the murder didn't happen. She reminds herself that to attempt murder and to not succeed would be the ruin of her and Macbeth. Then she hears a noise. She tells herself she put the daggers where her husband could find them. Surely he couldn't have missed. She says King Duncan reminded her of her own father. If it wasn't for the uncanny resemblance, she might have killed the King herself.

Then Macbeth enters the scene carrying knives splattered with blood. Lady Macbeth sees him and proudly addresses him as 'My husband '.

Macbeth says he's done it and he ask her if she heard anything. She replies that she heard an owl and some crickets. She asked if he said something. Macbeth wants to know when she's talking about. (Notice, at this stage in the play, the speeches between Lady Macbeth become very short. It shows how stressed they are.)

Macbeth asks his wife to listen and then ask her who was sleeping in the second bedroom. She replies that it is Donalbain. He then looks down at his bloody hands and calls them 'a sorry sight'. His wife says that's a silly thing to say.

Then Macbeth tells her that one of the servants laughed in his sleep, and one shouted out 'Murder!'. They woke each other up and then they went back to sleep after saying their prayers.

Lady Macbeth says the servants can rest in peace now that they've said their prayers, although some academics interpret the line about 'two lodged together' as to be about Malcolm and Donalbain sharing the same room. It seems more likely to be about the two servants that Macbeth is talking about. It was common practice in Elizabethan times the servants to share the same bed, so 'lodged together' probably refers to that as well as being 'laid to rest'.

Macbeth continues by saying that one servant cried out: 'God bless us!' While the other said: 'Amen'. He feels as if the servants saw his murderous hands. He says he couldn't say 'amen' when they said 'God bless us'. At this point, it is obvious that Macbeth feels like he has lost his religion.

Lady Macbeth tells them not to worry about it too much. But Macbeth still wants to know why he couldn't say 'amen'. He says the word stuck in his throat when he had desperate need of God's blessing.

Lady Macbeth says we can't think about it and that if they do they will lose their minds.

Macbeth then says he thought he heard somebody shout out: 'Sleep no more! Macbeth is killing sleep'. He is worried that innocent sleep, that can soothe away all the problems will never visit again.

Lady Macbeth ask him what he's talking about. He continues by saying he kept hearing the words: 'Sleep no more!' It seemed to be addressed to everybody in the house, but it specifically said that Macbeth will sleep no more.

Lady Macbeth asks who said that. She thinks that his strength is weakening. She tells them to get some water to wash the evidence from his hands. She asked him why did he take the daggers out of the room. They were supposed to stay next to Duncan. She tells him to take them back and smear the blood on the guards.

Macbeth says he can't go back. He's afraid to think about what he's done and can't stand to look at the grisly evidence of it.

Lady Macbeth is angry and thinks he is being cowardly. She tells him to give her the daggers. She reminds him that bed and sleeping people are not dangerous and that only children are afraid of them. She says she will put blood on the faces of the servants to make sure they appear to be guilty of the crime.

Lady Macbeth leaves and there is the sound of knocking from offstage. Macbeth is worried about whether knocking is coming from. He wonders what's happening to him, as he seems to be frightened of every noise. He looks at his hands and wonders who they belong to. He wonders if all the blood can be washed off by all the water in the oceans. He thinks the blood will turn their waters red.

Lady Macbeth returns and tells her husband that her hands are as red as his now. However, questioning his courage once more, she says her heart is not as white as husband's. The knocking sound continues in Lady Macbeth says the sound is coming from the south entrance. She says they should go back to their bedroom, but first he should simply wash away the evidence. She is annoyed as he seems to be in shock and unable to do anything.

The knocking continues. Lady Macbeth hears it and says that he should put on his nightgown, in case somebody sees them. She tells him to jump to it and stop being so absorbed in his thoughts.

Macbeth says he wishes he didn't know himself, so he didn't have to think about his crime.

The knocking continues and Macbeth says he wishes it could wake Duncan. Then he and Lady Macbeth leave the stage.

Act 2 Scene 3

This scene is often referred to as 'the porter scene'. It serves as the only comic interlude in what is a very bloody and gruesome play.

The drunken porter enters, and hearing the knocking says there is a lot of it. He says if he were opening the gates to hell he would be turning the key a lot. The knocking continues and the porter pretends he is Hell's gatekeeper, by saying: who's there in the devil's name? He wonders if it's a farmer who is killed himself because grain is too cheap. He tells the farmer he's just in time. He tells the imaginary farmer that he should have brought a lot of handkerchiefs with him, as you sweat a lot in Hell.

The knocking continues and the porter wonders who's there. This time he thinks it's a treasonous Jesuit, who's not sure if he should follow the Pope or the King. Anyway, he can't fool God, so he'd better come in too.

The knocking continues. This time the porter thinks it may be an English tailor, who used less fabric for people's clothes than he should of, trying to pass them off as tight French fashions. He tells the tailor he will be roasted like a goose. Presumably, this means on a spit.

The knocking continues, and the porter complains he never gets any peace. He says this place is too cold to be Hell, and he doesn't want to pretend to be the devil's porter anymore although he had intended to let people from all professions have the chance to come here.

The knocking continues, and the porter shouts impatiently that he's coming. He tells whoever it is to hold on, and not forget to give him a tip.

The porter then opens the gate for Macduff and Lennox to enter. Macduff begins by saying to the porter, was it because he went to bed so late that he struggled to get up now.

The porter replies they were drinking until 3 AM and that drink can do three things to a man.

Macduff ask what three things are, to which the porter replies, drink can: turn your nose red, put you to sleep, and make you go to the toilet. It can also turn you on sexually, but let you down. It can stimulate your desire, but your performance in bed will suffer. In truth, drink is like a Jesuit, thinking one thing and doing another.

Macduff says it seems as if the porter was under the influence of this lie, last night.

The porter admits that the drink got him right in the throat, but he was too strong for it. His legs went a bit wobbly, but he managed to get rid of the alcohol, possibly by vomiting.

Macduff ask the porter if his master is awake yet. At that moment, Macbeth appears on stage, and Macduff says that the knocking must have woken him up.

Lennox greets Macbeth, and the greeting is returned to both of them. Macduff asks Macbeth if the King is awake, to which he replies: 'Not yet.' Macduff says he's been told to wake the king early and already it is later than the time he wanted to get up.

Macbeth says he will take Macduff to Duncan. Macduff says that it is hard work to be a host to the King but it is also an honour. Macbeth says enjoyable work is not really work and points out the door to Duncan's bedroom. Macduff says he'll go and wake the King up and leaves the stage.

Lennox asks Macbeth if the king is leaving today. Macbeth replies that he is and that it has been arranged. Lennox continues by saying the night has been wild. Wind was blowing down the chimneys; people were hearing cries in the night and strange sounds. They could have even been an earthquake.

Macbeth agrees that it was a rough night. Lennox says he is too young to remember anything quite like that.

Macduff returns saying he is seen something horrific beyond belief. Macbeth and Lennox simultaneously ask what's wrong. To which, Macduff replies the worst possible thing has happened. He says it's like murder in a church.

Macbeth is confused, and Lennox wonders if Macduff is talking about the King. Macduff says they should go into the bedroom and see for themselves. He says they will be horrified. He doesn't want to talk about it. They should see it for themselves and then try to put it into words. (This is typical of Gothic literature, in that what has happened is so terrible that it's indescribable.)

Macbeth and Lennox leave the stage to look in the King's bedroom. Meanwhile, Macduff tells everyone to wake up and ring the alarm bell. He calls out Banquo, Donalbain and Malcolm. He tells to shake off sleep, which is a bit like death, and look at the real thing. He tells them to come and witness the horror. He says the bell should ring. The bell rings and Lady Macbeth enters. She wants to know what's happening and why she can hear the sound of a terrible trumpet, waking everyone up.

Macduff calls her 'gentle'and says this news is not suitable for her ears. He says the news is so bad it would kill her to hear it.

At this moment, Banquo enters and Macduff addresses him telling the king has been killed.

Lady Macbeth reacts in surprise, saying how terrible that is. She asked if it happened in her house.

Banquo says it would be terrible no matter where it happened. He begs Macduff to say that he's lying and that it hasn't happened at all.

Macbeth and Lennox return, and Ross also enters. Macbeth says he wishes he had died an hour before this happened. He says nothing is worth living for now. He says all the wine has gone and there are only the dregs in the bottom left to drink.

Duncan's two sons, Malcolm and Donalbain enter. The latter asks what's wrong. Macbeth says Donalbain's wrong, but he doesn't know it yet. He says the source of their royal blood has come to an end.

Macduff put it more simply by saying their father has been murdered. Malcolm asks who did it.

Lennox says it seems the guards did it as their hands and faces were covered with blood. He adds that their daggers were also covered in blood. He says they looked confused, but they should not have been trusted with the life of the king.

Macbeth says he regrets killing the servants, nonetheless. Macduff asks why he did that.

Macbeth says it is always possible to be wise after the event when you're calm. He says it was violent rage that caused them to do it. The contrast between the white skinned Duncan and the killers covered in gore caused him to act in haste.

Lady Macbeth suddenly calls for help. Macduff tells Macbeth to help his wife.

Malcolm speaks to his brother, Donalbain, in an aside. He asks why they are keeping quiet, when both of them have the most to say.

Donalbain replies that the situation is dangerous and that they should get out. He says they haven't even had time to grieve yet, but they will have plenty of time to do so. Malcolm says the time hasn't yet come for them to turn grief into action.

Banquo also says that someone should look after Lady Macbeth, who goes offstage with her attendants. He adds that when they're properly dressed the cold weather, they should meet to discuss what can be done. He says they are too shaken to make quick decisions. He says he'll put himself in God's hands, and fight against whatever caused this murder.

Macduff says he will too, as do everybody else on stage. Macbeth says they should get dressed quickly me in the hall. To that, everyone agrees.

Then, all the characters on stage exit, apart from Malcolm and Donalbain. Malcolm asks his brother what he's going to do. He says they should not stay here. He says it's easy for a line to pretend he feels grief, when he actually feels none at all. He tells Donalbain that he's going to England.

Donalbain says he'll go to Ireland (which seems a bit of a strange place to go, given that some Irish soldiers were involved in the rebellion against his father). He tells

Malcolm they will be safer if they go in different directions. He says wherever they go, men will smile at them while holding daggers at the same time. He says they should beware people that are closest to them. Malcolm says they haven't yet come across that kind of danger, so the best thing to do would be to avoid it. He says they should jump on their horses, and not worry about saying polite goodbyes. And off they ride.

Act 2 Scene 4

Ross enters with an old man, who reminisces about how it was 70 years ago. The man says he's seen a lot of terrible things but last night's horrors take the biscuit! Ross replies that your man can see 'the heavens', which must look upset with what man is doing below. The weather is appalling, which suggests that heaven is angry. Although it is daytime it looks as black as night.

The old man said it's as unnatural as the murder of the King. He mentions that last Tuesday a fork and was killed by an owl, that usually only preys on mice.

Ross says something just as strange happened: Duncan's horses escaped. His tame horses seemed to be at war with everyone .

The old man says he heard about that. He even heard the horses ate, or bit. Each other.

Ross says he saw it with his own eyes and he couldn't believe it. He tells the old man that Macduff is coming. Macduff duly enters and Ross asked him how things are. Macduff asks Ross if he cannot see for himself. To this, Ross asked Macduff if anybody knows who committed the murder?

Macduff replies it was the servants, who were killed by Macbeth. Ross says it's a shame that Macbeth did that.

He can't understand what would motivate them to do such a thing.

Macduff says they were paid to do it. Malcolm and Donalbain, the king's sons, have fled; so now they are the prime suspects.

Ross complains everything is unnatural. He says how stupid it is that a son can kill the father that supports him. He says Macbeth will probably become king now.

Macduff says Macbeth has already been named king and has gone to Scone to be crowned.

Ross asks Macduff where Duncan's body is. Macduff replies that it is in Colmekill, on the tiny island of Iona in the Hebrides, which is the holy resting place for Scottish kings.

Ross asks if Macduff will also go to Scone, but Macduff says he will go to Fife instead. Nevertheless, Ross says he will go on to Scone regardless.

Macduff wishes Ross well. He says things can't get much worse.

Ross says goodbye to the old man, who in return blesses him. Then they all leave the stage.

Act 3 Scene 1

Banquo enters and says that Macbeth has everything: he's king, thane of Cawdor and also thane of Glamis, just like the witches predicted. He thinks Macbeth may have cheated to get all of these titles. However, he remembers that Macbeth's descendents would not become kings. Instead, it would be Banquo's descendents that would become kings. He hears a noise, so he is suddenly quiet. Then a sound of a trumpet is heard, before Macbeth enters, dressed as King of Scotland. Lady Macbeth enters dressed as his queen. Lennox, Ross, lords, ladies and attendants also enter.

Macbeth notices Banquo and, pointing to him, says he is the most important guest. Lady Macbeth adds that no celebration would be complete without Banquo.
Macbeth speaks to Banquo saying that he wants him to attend the ceremonial banquet that night. Banquo says he will do whatever is commanded.
Macbeth asks Banquo if he's going riding that afternoon. Banquo says he is. Macbeth says he would have liked to have had Banquo's serious input at the council meeting that day, but it can wait until tomorrow then. He asks if Banquo is intending to ride a long way. Banquo says he'll ride until dinner time and expects to be back an hour or two after sunset.
Macbeth reminds him not to miss the feast and Banquo says he won't.
Macbeth goes on to say that he's heard that the princes have gone to England and Ireland respectively. He adds that they haven't yet confessed to the cruel murder of their own father. Instead, they are telling lies. He tells Banquo they can talk about that and other important things more tomorrow. He tells him to hurry up and get on his horse. He says he'll see him tonight. He asked him if his son, Fleance is going along with him.
Banquo says he is and it's time for him to go. Macbeth says he hopes that Banquo's horses are fast and not the type to trip up, before saying goodbye. When Banquo leaves.
Macbeth continues speaking. He says everyone can do what they want until seven o'clock tonight. To make society a better place, Macbeth will slink off by himself until suppertime, so he wishes everyone well until then. (He seems to be enjoying playing the role of villain, at this point.) Then, everyone exitts except Macbeth and a

servant, whom he speaks to. He asks the servant if 'those men' are waiting for him. The servant replies that they are waiting outside the palace gate. Macbeth tells servants go and get them and bring them in. So the servant leaves.

We, as an audience, discover Macbeth's inner thoughts as he delivers another soliloquy. In it, he says that it's not much good being the king if you are not safe. He is worried about Banquo. It's Banquo's noble nature that makes him afraid. Banquo is willing to take risks and he never stopped thinking. Banquo is brave but also plays it safe. Banquo is the one person that Macbeth is afraid of. He likens his position to that Mark Anthony, whose angel feared Octavius Caesar. He reminds himself how Banquo scolded the witches are calling Macbeth king, and how he asked them to tell him his future. That was when Banquo found out he would be the father to a number of kings. Consequently, Macbeth has a crown that he cannot pass on to the member of his family. If this is true, then he's holding 'a barren sceptre'. (This seems to be related to his seeming inability to father a son.) Also, murdering Duncan will mostly benefit Banquo's sons. Macbeth can have no peace of mind now. He has sold his soul to the devil so that Banquo's sons can be kings. Instead of that, Macbeth pledges he will fight Fate, if necessary, to the death. He hears somebody and asks who it is.

The servant returns with two murderers. Macbeth tells the servant to go to the door and stay there until he's called. Once the servant is gone Macbeth asks the murderers if it wasn't yesterday when they last spoke.

The first murderer says yes it was. So Macbeth continues, by asking him what he thought about what was said. He tells them that Banquo made their lives a misery for a long time. It wasn't Macbeth, although they thought it

was him at the time. He was innocent. He reminds them
that he showed in the proof in the last meeting and that he
explained how they were deceived. The evidence was so
overwhelming that even the halfwit would realise that
Banquo was guilty.

First murderer agrees that everything was revealed in
meeting. To which, Macbeth replies that more needs to
be done, which is why they are having a second meeting.
He asks the murderers if they are so patient that they
want Banquo's actions to go unpunished. He asked them
if they are so God-fearing that they want to pray for this
man who made them suffer so much.

The first murderer replies that they are simply men.
Macbeth agrees that they are part of species, as much as
everything from mongrels to pedigrees can be described
as dogs. He adds that if you list the different kinds of
dogs according to their qualities, you can tell which ones
are fast or slow, which ones are clever or dull-witted,
which ones are watchdogs and which ones are hunters.
Likewise, Macbeth claims you can classify men. He says
if the murderers are not at the very bottom of the list, then
they should let him know. If that is the case, he has a plan
to get rid of their enemy and make him happy. Macbeth
says he'll be sick as long as Banquo is alive. Things will
improve once he's dead.

At this, the second murderer speaks up. He says he's been
knocked about by the world has become so angry that it
will take any risk to get revenge.

The first murderer agrees. He says he's so sick of the bad
luck he's had that he'll take any risk to improve his life.
Macbeth reminds them that Banquo was their enemy, to
which they agree. Macbeth continues by telling them that
Banquo is his enemy too. Every moment of Banquo is

alive affects Macbeth negatively. As king, Macbeth has
the power to simply do away with Banquo. However,
they have friends in common that Macbeth still needs.
That's why he needs their help. He has to keep the public
from knowing about his plans to kill Banquo.

The second murderer tells Macbeth that they will do what
he wants them to. The first murderer adds that they are
prepared to sacrifice their lives.

Macbeth interrupts them by saying he can see their
fighting spirit shining through. He tells them that within
one hour he will let them know exactly where to go and
when to strike. He says it must be done tonight and not
too near the palace. He reminds them that he must be
suspected. They need to both Banquo and his son. He
tells them to each make up their own minds about it and
that he will come and see them soon.

Both murderer say in unison that they have decided that
they are going to do it. Macbeth says he will contact them
soon and they should stay inside the palace for now. Then
they leave the scene.

Macbeth continues to talk to himself. He says the deal is
done and Banquo so will be flying to heaven tonight.
Then he leaves the scene as well.

Act 3 Scene 2

Lady Macbeth enters with a servant. She asked the
servant if Banquo has left the court. The servant answers
that he has but he'll be back tonight. She asks the servant
to tell her husband that she wants to say a few words to
him. The servant says she will and exits.

Lady Macbeth speaks to herself saying if you get what
you want in your still unhappy, then you've spent
everything and gain nothing. She thinks it's better to be

person who is murdered, rather than the killer who is racked with guilt.

Mabeth arrives and she speaks to him. What's happening, she asks, why are you keeping yourself to yourself? Sad thoughts should die with the people you were worried about. If you can't sort it out, don't worry any more. What's done is done.

Macbeth says they have slashed the snake with a knife, but they haven't killed it yet. The snake will heal itself and be as threatening as before. Both heaven and earth will affected, while meals will be eaten in fear and sleep will be disrupted by nightmares. Macbeth feels he'd be better off dead. Duncan's sound asleep underground and nothing worse can happen to him now.

Lady Macbeth tells her husband to try to look relaxed and happy, as they are entertaining guests tonight.

Macbeth says he will. He hopes his wife can do the same. He tells her to give Banquo special attention and make him feel important. Flattery can do a lot to a lot to hide their true feelings.

Lady Macbeth tells her husband to stop talking this way, but he says his mind is 'full of scorpions'. In other words, he is suffering great mental anguish while Banquo and Fleance live.

Lady Macbeth says the pair won't live forever, but Macbeth says he takes comfort from the fact that they can be killed. That's why she should be cheerful. This dreadful deed will be completed before the bat flies through the castle and the dung beetle sings.

Lady Macbeth asks her husband what he's going to do. Macbeth says she's better off not knowing until after it's done. Then she can clap! He then speaks to the night, almost like a witch, saying keep the day in the dark so the bloody hand is invisible. Then he speaks to himself, saying it's getting dark and the crow is returning to the woods. Gentle creatures are beginning to sleep, while their nocturnal predators are waking up. He speaks to Lady Macbeth next, saying that she seems shocked, but she should not question him yet. The best way to complete bad deeds is to do more bad things. He asks her to accompany him and off the go.

Act 3 Scene 3

The two murderers enter with a third murderer, and the first one wants to know who told the third murderer to join them. The third murderer answers it was Macbeth. The second murderer says they shouldn't distrust in the third murderer as they are there for the same purpose.

The first murderer then tells the third murderer to stay with them. He says it's not night yet, and travellers are hurrying to get home or find somewhere to stay the night. Meanwhile, Banquo will be there soon.

The third murderer says he hears horses and then the audience hear Banquo calling from offstage that he need some light. Ironically, his light is about to be put out.

The second murderer says it must be Banquo as the rest of Macbeth's guests are inside the palace.

The first murderer says you can hear the horses and the third murderer says it's almost a mile to the palace gate, but Banquo is likely to leave his horses there and walk the rest of the way to the palace.

Then Banquo and Fleance enter with a torch, which the second murderer sees and mentions to his murderous colleagues. The third murderer identifies Banquo. The first murderer tells the others to get ready.

Banquo then says it's going to rain, and the first murderer interjects by saying: 'Let it come down.' At this point the murderous attack Banquo, who tells his son to flee. Banquo is killed and Fleance escapes.

The third murderous asks who put the light out. First murderer says wasn't it for the best? The third murderer points out that only one person has been killed and the son has escaped. The second murderer says they've failed in the 'best half' of their mission. To which, the first murderer says they should get going and tell Macbeth exactly what they did accomplish.

Act 3 Scene 4

This is often known as the banquet scene. Macbeth , Lady Macbeth, Ross, Lennox, Lords and attendants enter.

Macbeth tells the assembled throng that they know where they should sit, according to rank. From top to bottom, he welcomes all of them. Then they all sit down.

The lords thank Macbeth, who tells them that he will mingle amongst them. Meanwhile, his wife will stay seated until a more suitable time.

Lady Macbeth tells her husband to say 'welcome' to everyone on her behalf.

Then the first murderer appears at the door.

Macbeth continues talking to the guests. He says they are saying thank you to Lady Macbeth. As the table is full on both sides, he will sit in the middle and soon they will propose a toast. Then he goes to the door to meet the murderer, telling him there's blood on his face.

The first murderer says it must be Banquo's. Macbeth is pleased the blood is outside Banquo's body. He asks if Banquo has been killed.

The first murderer tells Macbeth that he cut Banquo's throat himself.

Macbeth compliments the murderer, saying he's the 'best' of the 'cutthroats'. Whoever did the same to Fleance is the best of the best.

The first murderer admits that Fleance has escaped. Macbeth's response is to say that he is having a fit, or a nervous breakdown, again. The news has imprisoned him in fear. He asks again about Banquo.

The first murderer says that Banquo is dead in a ditch with 20 deep gashes in his head. Macbeth thanks him for that. He says the adult snake is dead but the smaller version, or worm, has fled. That worm has no fangs at the moment. He tells the murderer to go and come back tomorrow. The murderer leaves.

Lady Macbeth tells Macbeth off for not entertaining his guests. To that, Macbeth says he's glad that she's reminded him, and he raises a toast to his guests. He says good digestion depends on a good appetite and good health depends on both.

Lennox invites Macbeth to take his seat, but the ghost of Banquo enters and sits in Macbeth's place. Macbeth says that if only Banquo were there all the nobility in Scotland would be under one roof. He says he hopes his being rudely delayed rather than the victim of something unfortunate.

Ross says that Banquo's absence means that he's broken his promise. Like Lennox, Ross invites Macbeth sit with them.

Macbeth replies and tables is full. Lennox says there is an empty seat, which has been reserved for Macbeth. As he can't see it, Macbeth asks where it is. Lennox points to whether ghost is sitting and then ask Macbeth what's wrong.

Macbeth demands to know who has done it. The lords don't know what he's talking about and in Macbeth talks to the ghost, telling it not to shake its head at him as he didn't do it.

Ross tells everyone to stand up because Macbeth is clearly unwell. But Lady Macbeth tells all of them to sit down again, as Macbeth has often been like this since he was a youth. She calls it a 'momentary' fit. She tells them not pay attention to Macbeth, or they will make his condition worse. Then, in a private aside to a husband, she asks him if he is a man.

Macbeth replies that he is brave, if he dares to look at something that would even scare the devil.

Lady Macbeth says that's nonsense and just one of his hallucinations that he gets when he scared, just like the floating dagger he saw. She says he is more like a woman telling a scary story by the fire in front of her grandmother. She says he should be ashamed of himself making silly faces. When he calms down, you will notice is just looking at a stool. It's an interesting use of language there, as Shakespeare may be saying that Macbeth is looking at excrement and finding more in it than meets the eye. It's a typical sign of madness.

Macbeth cleans without to go over and look for herself. He then speaks to the ghost and asks it what it has to say. He tells it if it can nod then it should speak too. If the dead are going to return like this then there's no point burying anybody. Instead we should let the kites eat our dead. The ghost disappears.

Lady Macbeth asks her husband if he is completely paralysed by his foolish fears. Macbeth replies that he saw the ghost as surely as he is standing before her now.

Lady Macbeth tells him it's shameful nonsense. In response, Macbeth tells her about ancient times when a lot of blood was spilled. He adds that since then, other terrible murders in committed. Before, those murdered used to simply die and that would be the end of it. But now, even a man with 20 fatal head wounds can reappear and knock us off our stools. That's stranger than murder. Lady Macbeth reminds her husband that his friends are missing him. Macbeth admits he forgot about them. Then he speaks to his guests, telling them not to be alarmed. He says she has a strange mental illness, which is only shocking if you don't know him. He then raises his glass to toast the assembled throng, saying he wants to toast 'love and health to all'. He says he will sit down now only ask for some wine. He tells them to fill up his cup.

But the ghost of Banquo reappears in Macbeth seat. Macbeth doesn't notice at first, and he says he drinks to the happiness of everyone there and to Banquo. He says he wishes he were here. The Lords agree with the toast, and they all drink.

At this point, Macbeth notices the ghost. She tells it to get out of his sight and stay in its grave. He says it has no marrow in its bones and its blood is cold. He says it's staring at him with eyes that have no power to see.

Lady Macbeth talks to the guests, who are obviously startled. She chosen to think of it as nothing more than a strange habit. She says it's nothing more than that, although it does spoil the moment.

Macbeth says he is as brave as any other man. He invites the ghost to come in the form of a Russian bear, or rhinoceros, or an Iranian tiger. He says that would be much less scary. Or he invites the ghost to come back and challenging to a duel in a deserted place with a sword. If he trembles then, it would be fair to call him a little girl. He tells the horrible shadow to disappear as it's only an hallucination. The ghost vanishes.

Macbeth says he is a man once again, so asks everybody to remain seated.

Lady Macbeth says he has ruined the party by making a spectacle of himself.

Macbeth then talks to the guests. He asked them if things like this can happen without making everyone so astonished. He says they make him feel as if he doesn't know himself, when he looks at these terrible things that make him white with fear while they are unaffected.

Ross asks him what things. Lady Macbeth tells them not to speak to him. She says he will only get worse by talking. She advises them to leave immediately, not in rank order, but just to go.

Lennox says good night and wishes the king a speedy recovery. Lady Macbeth wishes them good night too, and everyone leaves except for her and her husband.

Macbeth then says there is an old proverb which says the murdered will get their revenge. Gravestones can move and trees can speak if it brings justice. Crows and magpies have even exposed murderers before. Then he asks his wife what time it is that night.

She replies it's almost morning, but you can't tell if it's day or night. He asks what she thinks about the fact that Macduff deciding that he won't obey the king. Lady Macbeth asks if he sent for Macduff.

Macbeth says not exactly, but he will send him. He explains that he has spies in Macduff's house. He says tomorrow he will go to visit the witches again. He is determined to find out the worst about the future. He says returning to being good would be just as hard as to keep telling people. He says he has a few ideas that he once put into action before he thinks about them.

Lady Macbeth reminds her husband that he hasn't slept. He says sleep is a good idea. He thinks his delusions may be fuelled by his lack of killing experience. In that sense, they are both just beginners. They both go to bed.

Act 3 Scene 5

There is the sound of thunder as the three witches enter, meeting Hecate.

The first witch ask Hecate what's wrong, as she seems to be angry.

Hecate replies that she has good reason. She dismissively calls them presumptuous hags. She wants to know why they've given Macbeth riddles and prophecies about his future without consulting her first. She reminds them that she is their controller. To make matters worse, they've done this for a perverse young male, who is unlikely to do anything for them in return. She says they can repair the damage by meeting her at Acheron (which is a Greek mythological name of a river in hell) in the morning. She says Macbeth will go there to find out about his future. She tells to bring everything with them that they need to make magic. Meanwhile, she'll fly away and work on some horrible spell. She chosen she has a lot to do before noon, as she has to catch a droplet from the moon, which will help produce magic to trick Macbeth. This magic will fool Macbeth into thinking he is more important than fate itself. He will think he is above everything, and complacency is the greatest enemy of mortal human beings.

Suddenly music is heard, with voices singing: 'Come away'. Hecate says she is being called away and her little spirit is sitting in a foggy cloud waiting for her. Then she leaves.

The first witch tells the other two to hurry and leave as well, as Hecate will be back soon. Then they all go.

Act 3 Scene 6

This scene begins with Lennox and another Lord entering. Lennox says that what he said already shows they are on the same wavelength. Strange things have been going on. He says Macbeth pitied Duncan, but that was after he was dead. Banquo was out too late at night, and some may say Fleance killed him as he left the scene of the crime. The moral is not to walk too late at night. And how could Malcolm Donalbain kill their own father? Macbeth grieved Duncan's death and killed the drunken servants immediately. That was the right thing to do, wasn't it? It was probably wise too, as it would have been even more outrageous to hear the two of them deny what they had done. All in all, Lennox feels Macbeth has handled a difficult situation well. If only all the murdering sons could be rounded up and put in prison, then they would find out exactly how awful punishment can be he say. Lennox ends by saying that he can hear the out-of-favour Macduff arriving. It wasn't a good idea for him not to show up at 'the tyrant's feast'. Now Macduff has to hide. He asks the Lord where he's hiding.

The Lord responds by saying that Duncan's son, Malcolm, lives in Edward the Confessor's royal court in England. Macduff went there too to ask King Edward for help. He hopes to form an alliance with the Lord of Northumberland, Siward. With their help, Macduff hopes to return peace to Scotland. Meanwhile, Macbeth has heard the news and is so angry that he is preparing for war.

Lennox asks if Macbeth told Macduff to return to Scotland. To this, the Lord replies that he did. Macduff told the messenger there was no way he would return. The messenger turned his back on Macduff and made him feel that he will regret his decision.

Lennox muses that that may well keep Macduff away from Scotland. However, he believes that someone should tell Macduff to return and free Scotland, which is now under the rule of a tyrant!

The Lord says he will pray for that. Then they both go.

Act 4 Scene 1

The sound of thunder opens the scene and in it we can see a boiling cauldron inside a cavern. The three witches enter.

The first witch says the tawny brown cat has meowed three times, and the second witch says the hedgehog as whined once. The third which says her familiar is telling them to get on with the magic.

The first witch says they should dance around the cauldron and throw in poisoned entrails. She throws in a poisonous toad first. Then the witches chant together: 'Double, double toil and trouble'.

The second witch wants to boil a slice of snake, taken from the fens, or marshes, or bogs. She wants to throw in a lot of other magic ingredients too. The witches chant again.

The third witch wants to add even more unwholesome ingredients, finishing off with a tiger's entrails. They chant in unison once again.

Then the second witch says they'll cool it down with baboon blood. Then it will be finished.

Now Hecate enters along with three other witches and tells them what a good job they've done. She says all of

them will share the rewards and she invites them to sing around the cauldron. Music begins to play the six witches sing a song entitled 'Black Spirits'. Hecate leaves.
The second witch says she knows something wicked is coming, as her thumbs are tingling. She says they must open the doors for whoever knocks.
Macbeth enters and ask them what they're doing, describing them as 'secret, black , and midnight hags'. They replied there is no word to describe what they've done.
Macbeth says he wants some answers to his questions in the name of whoever they serve. He doesn't care about all the terrible things they can do just wants to know the answers to his questions.
The first witch tells him to speak. The second witch also. The third witch says they'll answer his questions. Then the first witch ask him if he would rather hear the answers from their mouths or from their masters'.
Macbeth says they should call their masters, and then he'll see.
Now the first witch pours the blood of a female pig into the cauldron. And she adds even more ingredients. All the witches chant, telling their masters to show themselves.
There is the sound of thunder and the first apparition is a head wearing a helmet. Macbeth speaks to it, beginning to ask a question. But the first witch says, the apparition can read keep his mind, so Macbeth should just listen and not speak.
The first apparition tells Macbeth to beware Macduff, the Thane of Fife. He then asks to go. He descends into the ground or the cauldron.

Macbeth thanks the apparition, saying he guessed as much. He asked for one more word of advice. The first which says the apparition will not be commanded. However, another one is coming who is stronger than the first.

We hear thunder again, and a second apparition appears which looks like a bloody child. It calls out Mac beth's name three times, to which he replies that he would listen with all three ears if he had them.

The second apparition continues by telling Macbeth to be strong. He can laugh at the power of other men, has nobody born from a woman can ever hope to hurt him. The second apparition also descends.

Macbeth concludes that he doesn't need to kill Macduff and has no reason to feel afraid of him. Nonetheless, he wants to make doubly sure by killing Macduff. At least then he can sleep better at night.

Sound of Thunder is heard again, and the third apparition appears. This one looks like a child with a crown on its head. It is holding a tree in its hand. Macbeth asks what it is.

All the witches tell him to listen but not speak to it. The third apparition tells Macbeth to be brave like a lion and proud. It tells him not to worry about who is conspiring against him. It tells him he will never be defeated until Birnam Wood marches to fight him at Dunsinane Hill. Then it descends.

Macbeth says that will never happen. How can the trees pulled their roots out of the earth and march? He considers that the apparitions have said to be good omens. But he wants another one more question: will Banquo's sons ever reign in Scotland.

The witches tell him not to ask any more questions. Macbeth says if they don't answer then he will curse them. He asked why the cauldron sinking and what the noise is.

The music of hautboys is heard. Each of the three original witches says 'Show', before they all chant in unison: 'Show his eyes and grieve his heart'. Then eight kings march across the stage, with the last one holding the mirror. They are followed by Banquo.

Macbeth says that spirit looks too much like the ghost of Banquo. He tells it to go away. He asks the which is why they are showing him this. In the mirror he can see many more men. Some of these future kings are kings of more than one country. And to make it even worse, Banquo is smiling and pointing at them. He asks if this is a true prophecy.

The first witch says it's true, but there's no point looking so confused. She then tells her sisters to try to cheer Macbeth up by dancing and showing him 'the best' of their 'delights'. Music plays, they dance and then they vanish.

Macbeth wonders where they've gone. He says this hour will be marked in the calendar as cursed. He calls to somebody off stage to come in and Lennox enters.

Lennox asks Macbeth what he wants. To that, Macbeth asks Lennox if he saw the witches. Lennox says he didn't. Macbeth ask Lennox if they passed by him. Lennox says they didn't. Macbeth says the air they ride upon is infected, and he damns everyone who trusts them. Ironically, he trusts himself. He could swear he heard the galloping of horses. He asks Lennox who has come.

Lennox says its two or three men reporting that Macduff has fled to England. Macbeth can hardly believe his ears, so Lennox has to confirm the news.

Macbeth thinks his plans had been anticipated. He complains that if you don't do something immediately when you think of it, you might not get a chance to do it. He now promises to act on impulse. The next thing he wants to do is raid Macduff's castle, seize the town of Fife, kill Macduff's wife and his children and anyone else who could inherit Macduff's wealth. He swears he will do this before he cools down. He's had enough of apparitions, he wants to meet the messengers. He tells Lennox to bring them to him. Then they go.

Act 4 Scene 2

Lady Macduff, her son and Ross enter. She asks what did husband do to make him leave Scotland?

Ross tells her to be patient, but she replies that her husband had no patience. She thinks she was mad to run away. Even if you're not a traitor, fear can make you look like one.

Ross says it's hard to tell whether it was wisdom or fear that made him run to England. But lady Macbeth can't believe it's wisdom to leave his wife and children and his house and titles in an unsafe place. She concludes that he doesn't love his family as you has no instinct to look after them. She mentions how the smallest of birds will fight against the owl, if it threatens its young. Her husband is fearful and that's why he's run away. There is no wisdom in it.

Ross tells her to compose herself. He reiterates that her husband is noble, wise and judicious. He says it's not safe for him to say too much, but times are bad if nearly everybody is being accused of being a traitor. He likens it to being tossed around in an ocean and getting nowhere. He says he will leave now but come back shortly. He says when things are bad it will either stop or improve to the way it was. He then blesses Lady Macduff.

Talking about her child, Lady Macduff says he's now fatherless. Ross reminds he has to go before he starts crying. Then he leaves.

Lady Macduff tells her son that his father's death. She asked him how he's going to live now.

The son replies that he will live like a bird. She asks him if he means eating worms and flies. He says he means he will live on whatever he can. She says she would easily be trapped as he doesn't understand fear. That's ironic, as she has accused her husband of being too fearful. Perhaps Macduff has more of the survival instinct in him than his son, who says hunters won't want him. The son also says his father is not dead, no matter what she says.

Lady Macduff insists that her husband is dead. She asked her son what he would do for a father. The son says what should she do about the husband. She says she can buy twenty. He says you'll sell them again. Lady Macduff commences his wit.

The son asks his mother his father was a traitor. Lady Macduff says he was. Then the son asks for a definition. She says it's someone who makes a promise and breaks it. He asked her if that applies to everyone. She says yes and they should all be hanged. He wants to know who should hang them, and his mother replies 'honest men'. He can't understand how the honest men can hang the dishonest men, as there are far more of the latter in this world. She laughs at his joke, but then repeats her question about what he would do without a father.

The boy says he cannot be dead, as otherwise his mother would be crying. The fact that she is not crying is a good sign that he will have a new father soon. She calls him a silly chatterbox.

Then a messenger enters. He tells Lady Macduff and something terribly dangerous is coming. He tells not to be here when it arrives. The chosen to go away immediately and take children. Then he goes as he fears for his own safety.

Lady Macbeth ask where she should go. She says she's done nothing wrong. But she says it's quite womanly to say that.

Then the murderers enter and she says who are these people. The first murderer asks her where her husband is. She says she hopes he is not anywhere where they can find him. The first murderer calls Macduff traitor, to which the son says it's a lie. The first murderer stabs the son. He says he has been killed and urges his mother to run away. She runs offstage screaming 'murder!' but is pursued by the murderers, while her son dies onstage.

Act 4 Scene 3

Malcolm and Macduff enter, with the former saying they should find a shady place where they can sit down and cry.

Macduff says insulin crying and should defend their homeland with their swords. Each day there are new widows, orphans and sorrows. Scotland is crying out in pain.

Malcolm says he will fix all of this when the time is right. He says he can't even speak the name of the tyrant, especially as Macbeth was once considered to be honest. He thinks Macduff is a favourite of Macbeth and is uninjured so far. For all Malcolm knows, Macbeth could have sent Macduff south to trap him.

Macduff simply says that he's not treacherous. To that, Malcolm replies that Macbeth is, though. He adds that even a virtuous person will do what his King tells him to. Even the brightest angel, Lucifer, fell from grace.

Macduff says he's lost hope in convincing Malcolm to fight on his side against Macbeth. Malcolm says the hope was lost in his doubts about him. He asks him why he left his wife and child behind. He tells them not to misinterpret his suspicions and to just give honest answers.

Macduff says the country is bleeding because of the tyrant. He says he cannot be corrupted by him, not for all the riches in the world.

Malcolm tells Macduff not to be offended. He agrees that Scotland is sinking under Macbeth rule and that the country is crying and bleeding. He thinks he could raise an army, as the English and promised him thousands of troops. But even if he can end Macbeth rule, how can he be sure the country will be better off than before. Perhaps it will suffer a worse fate, once a new king is in place.

Macduff can't understand what he means exactly, so Malcolm explains that he is talking about himself. He says Macbeth will seem as pure as snow in comparison.

Macduff says no one is worse than Macbeth. To that, Malcolm admits that Macbeth is murderous and evil in so many ways. But Malcolm says his sexual desires are such that no woman would be safe in Scotland if he were king. Therefore it would be better for Macbeth to rule.

Macduff replies that endless greed and lust is a kind of tyranny in itself, which is caused the downfall of many kings. But the throne belongs to Malcolm. He should find a way to satisfy his desires in secret, while appearing virtuous on the surface. There are plenty of women for a king if he wants them.

Malcolm says he is also greedy. He will take land from the nobles, jewels and houses to. He would invent false quarrels if he had to just to get more wealth.

Macduff says greed is worse than lust, as he will never grow out of it. However, Scotland has enough treasure to satisfy him, if he becomes king. Anyway, he must have good sides.

Malcolm says he doesn't have a good side. He says he lacks all the qualities that a king needs. All he has is vices.

Macduff calls out the name of his country in frustration. Malcolm says if Macduff thinks he's fit to be king he should let him know.

Macduff says he must be joking, as he's not fit to live let alone be king. Although his father Duncan was virtuous, it seems as if Malcolm is anything but. Malcolm's mother was always praying, but all for nothing. Scotland's hope is dead, according to Macduff.

Then Malcolm says the passionate outburst has proved Macduff's integrity. Suddenly, Malcolm has no doubt that Macduff is trustworthy. He says he can't believe people because Macbeth has tried many times to trick him. Now, Malcolm says he will be guided by Macduff. He says he hasn't done any of the bad things that he claimed to have done. These are the first lies he's ever told and now he is ready to serve his country. He adds that before Macduff arrived, old Siward agreed to commit 10,000 soldiers for battle. Now they can join forces and increase their chances of success. He asks Macduff why he is so quiet.

Macduff says it's hard to make sense of two very different stories.

At this point, a doctor enters. Malcolm tells Macduff they'll speak more later and then he asks the doctor if King Edward is coming.

The doctor says King Edward is coming to offer cures to a bunch of sick people, who can be healed by him simply touching them. Malcolm thanks the doctor, who then leaves.

Macduff asked what kind of disease he is talking about, to which Malcolm replies 'evil'. Malcolm says he's seen Edward's miraculous powers of healing many times during his stay in England. This power will be inherited by his descendants. As well as that, Edward can prophesy the future. He is favoured by God.

Then Ross enters, and Macduff wonders who's coming. Malcolm says his clothes indicate that he is a Scotsman, buddy, recognise him.

Macduff welcomes the stranger, and Malcolm says he recognises him now. He says that been kept apart by circumstances and hopes that will change. Ross says he hopes so too.

Macduff asks Ross if Scotland is in the same situation. Ross replies that the countries to afraid to even look at itself. It's not the place they were born in, but it is the place still die in.

Macduff says the report is poetic, yet it sounds true. Malcolm asked about the recent news, to which Ross replies that awful things happen every minute.

Macduff asks about his wife, but Ross says she is well, as are his children. He says at least they were when he left them. Macduff asks Ross to expand on that, so he says he heard rumours that good men are ready to rebel against

Macbeth. Even women would fight if Malcolm and
Macduff join the rebellion.
Malcolm tells Ross that he is returning to Scotland with
Lord Siward, a very experienced Christian soldier, and
10,000 troops.
Ross wishes he had some good news to respond with.
Instead he has the kind of news that should be 'howled
out in the desert air' where no one can hear it.
Macduff wants to know exactly what it's about. Does it
affect everyone or just one of them?
Ross says no decent person can be immune from sorrow,
but the main part of the bad news affects Macduff.
To that, Macduff responds by saying he would like to
know immediately. Ross warns Macduff that this news
will be the worst he's ever heard. Macduff says he thinks
he can guess what that is. Then Ross reveals that
Macduff's castle was attacked and his wife and children
savagely slaughtered. He is afraid to reveal more details
in case it results in the death of Macduff.
Malcolm shouts to the heavens and then to Macduff,
telling him not to keep his grief to himself. Malcolm tells
Macduff to put his grief into words, otherwise it will be
too much to bear for his heart.
Macduff asks if his children were killed too. To this, Ross
replies that his wife, his children, his servants and
everyone else who could be found were murdered.
Macduff complains that he was away when it happened.
He asked again if his wife was killed too. Ross replies
that he's already said that she was.
Malcolm tells Macduff to be comforted by the thought of
revenge on Macbeth. However, Macduff says Macbeth
doesn't have children. He asks again if all his pretty
children and his wife died in one fell swoop.

Malcolm urges him to fight like a man, but Macduff says he has to feel it like a man first. He feels very sorry because his family didn't do anything wrong. He hopes they can rest in peace.

Malcolm tells Macduff to let younger sharpen his sword. Grief can be converted into anger.

Macduff says he could go on crying like a woman and bragging about revenge. He doesn't want to wait. He wants to be face-to-face with Macbeth.

Malcolm says that Macduff now sounds like a man. He says they should go and see King Edward as the army is now ready and Macbeth is ripe for the picking. Doesn't cheer up as the day will dawn at last. Then they all go.

Act 5 Scene 1

A doctor and a waiting-gentlewoman enter.

The doctor says he stayed up late tonight announced so far haven't seen any evidence about Lady Macbeth sleepwalking.

The gentleman replies that since Macbeth went to war, Lady Macbeth has got out of bed, written something down while staying asleep and then returned to bed.

The doctor says it's unnatural to act as if you are awake when you're asleep. He asks if she's said anything. To that, the gentleman says she will not repeat it.

The doctor says he needs to know, but the gentlewoman says she will not tell anyone, as no one else witnessed it.

Lady Macbeth enters, holding a candle, and the gentlewoman says she's coming. The doctor asks how she got the candle. The gentlewoman replies it's by her bedside.

The doctor says Lady Macbeth's eyes are open, but the gentlewoman reminds him that she can't see anything. He asks her what she's doing now. She tells him Lady Macbeth is washing her hands.

Lady Macbeth speaks saying there's still a spot of blood on her hands. The doctor hears this and says he is going to write down what she says to help him remember better. Lady Macbeth rubs hands together and talks to the spot of blood. She commands it to leave. She mentions the mist or fog that awaits her in hell. It seems as if she is talking to her husband, as she addresses the air saying that it's nonsense. She can't understand why this imaginary person, who is a soldier, is afraid. She says they don't need to be, as their guilt cannot be proven. However, she is dismayed by the amount of blood that the old man had in him.

The doctor asks the gentlewoman if she heard that. Lady Macbeth continues her ranting and raving, by asking what happened to the Thane of Fife's wife. (Of course, she's talking about Lady Macduff.) She wonders if her hands will ever be clean. She then talks to the imaginary person, telling it to stop what it's doing and stop acting startled, as that will ruin everything.

The doctor tells the gentlewoman to go, as she's heard things that she shouldn't have.

The gentlewoman says that Lady Macbeth has said something she shouldn't have, and she's sure of that.

Lady Macbeth continues by saying she still has the smell of blood on her little hand. Even all the perfume of Arabia couldn't make it smell better. Then she sighs.

The doctor remarks on how she sighs, and thinks she is carrying a heavy burden on her heart. The gentlewoman says she wouldn't want a heart like that even if she were Queen. After some wordplay, the doctor says he cannot treat Lady Macbeth, as her mental illness is beyond his medical knowledge. He says he knows sleepwalkers who have died without any guilt to worry about.

Lady Macbeth continues by telling herself to wash your hands and put on her nightgown. It's almost as if she is out side of herself, as she addresses herself in the second person. She tells herself not to look pale. She tells herself that Banquo is buried and he cannot return.

The doctor asks if this is true.

Lady Macbeth continues telling herself to go to bed. She says she has a knocking at the gate. She tells herself to hold hands and not worry about what has been done, for it cannot be undone. Then she tells herself to go to bed before exiting.

The doctor asks if she will go to bed now, to which the gentlewoman says, yes, immediately. The doctor continues by saying their evil rumours are everywhere. Unnatural things can cause the supernatural to happen. Guilty people will confess in their sleep. He adds that Lady Macbeth needs a priest more than a doctor. He tells the gentlewoman to look after Lady Macbeth and remove anything that she might injure herself with. He tells her to keep constant watch on Lady Macbeth before wishing the gentlewoman good night. He says he has a strong opinion but doesn't want to say it aloud.

The gentlewoman wishes him good night and they both exit.

Act 5 Scene 2

We hear drums and we see flags. Menteith, Caithness, Angus, Lennox and soldiers enter with a Drummer.

Menteith says the English army is near. It is being led by Malcolm, his uncle Siward and Macduff. He says they motivated by revenge. That motivation is so strong it would even make dead men come alive.

Angus says they will meet the Armenia Birnam Wood, as that is the route they taking.

Caithness wants to know if Donalbain will be with his brother, Malcolm. Lennox replies that Donalbain is definitely not there. However, Siward's son will be one of the un-bearded men fighting in this battle, hoping to become fully fledged men. Interestingly, the witches have more of a beard than some of the soldiers.

Menteith asks what what Macbeth is doing, to which Caithness replies that Macbeth is fortifying his castle, making his defence is stronger. Although some say he's insane, others say he's bravely furious. One thing's for sure, he's completely lost control of himself.

Angus says that Macbeth must feel the blood from the secret murders sticking to his hands. Rebel armies are about to punish him for his breach of trust. The soldiers he commands do not love him. He's like a tiny thief wearing giants robes.

Menteith seems to have some sympathy as he thinks Macbeth senses are acting independently, in shock about what Macbeth's body has done.

Caithness says they should keep marching on to give their loyalty to somebody who deserves it, like Malcolm. If they pour out their own blood, they can help cure the country sickness.

Lennox adds that however much blood is needed will be given to water the royal flower, represented by Malcolm, and kill off the weeds, or Macbeth. He also urges them to march on and they exit marching.

Act 5 Scene 3

Macbeth, the doctor and attendants enter.

Macbeth says to the doctor don't bring me any more reports. I don't care if everyone deserts me. I won't be scared until Birnam Wood moves itself to Dunsinane. Malcolm was born from a woman. I was told by the spirits not to fear anyone that was born that way. So leave me now, fake stains and join up with the English. My mind and my heart will not shake with doubt or fear.

A servant enters an Macbeth immediately insults him, by saying he hopes the devil turns his stupid white skin black. Then he asks a servant why he looks like a frightened goose.

The servant replies that there are 10,000, and Macbeth interrupts asking if he means geese. The servant clarifies and says he means soldiers.

Macbeth tells the servant to go and pinch his cheeks to bring some colour back into his face. He calls him cowardly. He says the servant power face may frighten other people too. He asks him what soldiers, to which the servant replies the English army. Macbeth tells him to leave immediately, which is what he does.

Macbeth calls out to Seyton, a homonym for Satan, and tells him he's sick at heart. He says that the battle will either secure his position for ever or else it will see him lose his throne. He says he's lived long enough, and now he feels like a yellowing leaf in autumn. He says he cannot enjoy the gifts of old age, as all he expects are curses.

Seyton arrives and asks Macbeth what he wants. Macbeth asks him for news. Seyton says all reports have been confirmed. To the Macbeth says he'll fight on until all the flesh is hacked from his bones. Then he asks for his armour.

Seyton tells him he doesn't need it yet, but Macbeth he'll put it on anyway. He orders his attendance to send out more cavalry to scour the whole country and hang anyone spreading fear. Once again he asked for his armour, then he asks the doctor how Lady Macbeth is.

The doctor says Lady Macbeth is not sick, but she is troubled: she keeps seeing visions that stop her sleeping. Macbeth tells the doctor to cure her. He asks him whether or not he can treat the diseased mind. He asked the doctor if he can take away memories of sorrow. He suggests using some kind of antidote to raise all the troubling thoughts that are weighing heavily upon her.

The doctor says that can only be done by the patient. Then Macbeth becomes impatient, and says you might as well throw medicine to the dogs. He won't have anything to do with it. Once again he calls for his armour and also for his lance. He tells the doctor to send out the soldiers. He tells the doctor the thanes are running away. He tells the doctor to hurry up. He wonders if the doctor can figure out what's wrong with the country. If he could cure it, Macbeth will applaud him. He then says pull it off. It's difficult to tell whether he means that the armour should be taken off, or whether he means that the doctor should pull off a miracle and cure the country. The latter seems likely as he asks the doctor what drugs he would use and has he heard of any cures.

The doctor replies that the preparation for war certainly sounds like something he can hear.

Macbeth tells the doctor to bring the armour and follow him. He maintains he will not be afraid to die until Birnam Forest moves to Dunsinane.

At this point, the doctor says he wishes he were far away from Dunsinane. He says money alone would not tempt him back. Then they both exit.

Act 5 Scene 4

We hear drums and we see the colour of the flags before Malcolm, old Siward, young Siward, Macduff, Menteith, Caithness, Angus, Lennox, Ross and soldiers come marching in with the drummer and a flag.

Malcolm says he hopes the time is coming when people will be safe in their bedrooms.

Menteith says he has no doubt that will happen. Siward asks the name of the forest behind them, to which Menteith replies its Birnam Wood.

Malcolm says they should tell every soldier to break off a branch and hold it in front of him. That way they can camouflage themselves, so Macbeth will have less idea about how many there are of them. The soldiers shout in unison that they will do it.

Siward says they have no news apart from the fact that Macbeth is still in Dunsinane and won't stop them laying siege to the castle.

Malcolm says that Macbeth wants them to lay siege. He adds that a lot of Macbeth soldiers are deserting and they don't have the fight for a battle against Macbeth's enemies.

Macduff says that they shouldn't judge the situation until they achieve their objective. He suggests that they work hard and soldiers.

Siward says they'll find out soon what is theirs and what isn't. He says thoughts are speculative, but blows in battle are more certain. He suggests that they move forward. So the Army exits, marching ahead.

Act 5 Scene 5

Macbeth, Seyton and soldiers enter with a drummer and a flag.

Macbeth commands them to put the flags on the outer walls. He says the castle was so strong they can laugh at the siege. Those laying siege can sit out there until they die of hunger and disease. Had it not been for the huge number of deserters, they could have joined them in battle in front of the castle and beaten back to England. The cry of women is heard offstage and Macbeth asks what is. Seyton says its women crying, before exiting. Macbeth says he's almost forgotten what it feels like to be afraid. He says at one time he would have been afraid by shriek in the night and his hair stood up if he heard a ghost story. But now he's had so many horrors to endure, horrible things can startle him no more. At that point, Seyton returns. Aacbeth, presumably hears a cry, as he asks Seyton what was the cry for. His doctor reports the Queen is dead.

Macbeth says she would have died later anyway. It was bound to happen. Tomorrow, and tomorrow, and tomorrow. He says the days creep slowly until the end of time. Each day brings a fool closer to his death, when the candle goes out. Life is nothing more than poor actor, who performs on stage for an hour and then disappears forever. It's like a noisy and dramatic story told by an idiot that has no meaning. Then the messenger enters, and Macbeth asks him to tell him the news, quickly.

The messenger says he should say what he saw but he doesn't know how to say it. Macbeth tells him to spit it out.

The messenger says he was standing on the hill, when he thought he saw Birnam Wood move. Macbeth calls him a liar. The messenger says punish me if it's not true. He says again he's seen a moving forest.

Macbeth says to the messenger, if he's lying he will hang him from the nearest tree until he dies of hunger. If he's telling the truth, Macbeth doesn't care if the messenger does the same to him. Macbeth speaks to himself saying that his confidence is diminishing. Is beginning to doubt the lies that sounded like the truth, when he was told not to worry until Birnam Wood comes to Dunsinane. Now it's happening. They should prepare to fight and go out of the castle. If what the messenger says is true, there's no point running away or staying in the castle. He says he's getting tired of living now, and he would like to see the world plunged into chaos. He says ring the alarm bells, and let the wind blow. At least they can die with their armour on their backs. They all leave.

Act 5 Scene 6

Malcolm, old Siward, Macduff and the Army enter carrying branches, along with a drummer and a flag. Malcolm says we close enough now. Through your branches on the ground and shows the enemy who you really are. He tells his uncle Siward and his son to lead the first charge into battle. Macduff and Malcolm will do the rest, according to their tactics.

Siward wishes them good luck. He says if he meets Macbeth's army, he'd rather lose if they cannot fight. Macduff orders all the trumpets to be blown to announce the arrival of blood and death. Then they all exit.

Act 5 Scene 7

Trumpets sound and the noise of battle can be heard as Macbeth enters.

Macbeth says he's been tied to a stake and he can't run away. He's like a bear, being attacked for the amusement of others. He asks where is the man who wasn't born from a woman. That's the only man he needs to be afraid of.

Young Siward enters and asks Macbeth his name. Macbeth answers that he'll be frightened when he hears it. Young Siward says he won't be, even if his name was hotter than any in hell. Macbeth reveals his identity. Young Siward says there is no name he hates more. Macbeth says no name is more frightening. Young Siward says he's a liar and a disgusting tyrant. He'll speak to him with his sword. In the fighting that ensues, Young Siward is killed.

Macbeth says to the dead body of young Siward, that he was born from a woman and swords don't frighten him. Macbeth exits and Macduff enters the scene with trumpet and battle sounds continuing. Macduff says that the noises coming from over there. He shouts to Macbeth that he should show his face. He says if someone else kills Macbeth, the ghosts of Lady Macduff and his children will forever haunt Macduff. He says he can't be bothered to fight mercenaries, or soldiers who only fight for money. If you can't find Macbeth and put down his sword. He thinks Macbeth must be in the area where there's a lot of noise, as it sounds like there's an announcement going on. He only asks for the luck to find Macbeth, and no more than that.

Macduff exits and more battle noises are heard as Malcolm and old Siward enter. Siward says to now, he should come this way. He says the castle was been surrendered without a fight. Macbeth's soldiers are fighting on both sides, while the Thanes are fighting bravely. The battle was almost won and it seems like there's not much left to do.

Malcolm says the enemies are fighting as if they don't even want to hurt them. Siward suggests they enter the castle. As they both exit, the battle noise continues.

Act 5 Scene 8

Macbeth enters and says why should he commit suicide like an ancient Roman. Instead he would prefer to see his enemy suffering wounds than himself.

Macduff enters and tells Macbeth to turn around, calling him a dog. Macbeth says to Macduff that he's the only man he has avoided. Macbeth says he feels guilty for killing all of Macduff's family, so he should go away. Macduff says he has nothing to say and his sword will do the talking. He says there are no words to describe how evil Macbeth is. Then they fight.

Macbeth says to Macduff that he's wasting his time trying to wound him. He might as well stab the air. Macbeth ranks that he lives a charmed life and he cannot be harmed by anyone from a woman.

Macduff tells Macbeth to forget about his charm. The evil spirit could have told Macbeth that Macduff is not born from a woman. He tells Macbeth that he was a Caesarean section birth.

Macbeth curses Macduff for telling him. He says his courage has melted away, but he doesn't believe that evil witches anymore. They tricked him with double meanings, raising his hopes before destroying them. He says he won't fight with Macduff.

They Macduff says that Macbeth should surrender. He says they'll put him in a freak show with unusual monsters.

Macbeth says he's not going to surrender and kiss the ground in front of Malcolm's feet. He won't suffer the humiliation of being taunted by common people. He will fight to the end and put up his shield. He tells Macduff to try to kill him if he dares. The first man to stop fighting will be damned forever. They exit the stage still fighting. Trumpets and battle noises continue. They re-enter

fighting and then Macbeth is slain. One Army's trumpet
sounds the call to retreat while the other sounds the call
of victory. Malcolm, Siward, Ross, the thanes and the
soldiers all enter with a drummer and a flag.
Malcolm says she wishes all his friends could have
survived this battle.
Siward replies that in every battle some people will be
casualties. He says judging by the men he can see, the
victory didn't cost very much in terms of lives.
Malcolm says that Macduff is still missing, as his young
Siward.
Ross says that young Siward is paid to soldiers price,
which is death. Young Siward only lived long enough to
become a man, and as soon as he proved his manhood by
fighting he died.
Siward asks for confirmation of his son's death. To that,
Ross says young Siward has been carried off. Ross adds
that if the grief were equal to young Siward is worth, the
sorrow would be never ending.
Checking for potential cowardice, Siward asks whether
the wounds were on his front, to which Ross replies they
were.
Siward describes his son as God's soldier now. He says
no son could have died more honourably.
Malcolm says that young Siward is worth more sorrow
and he will mourn for his death.
Siward says he is not worth more than that. His son died
well, and paid his dues. He hopes God is now with him.
He says it looks like better news is coming.
At that, Macduff enters carrying Macbeth's head.
Macduff greets Malcolm as king, as that is what he is
now. He says he has Macbeth's head and now they are
free from his tyranny. He says all the Lords of Scotland

want the same thing and they want to pronounce you king of Scotland. In unison they all chant: 'Hail, King of Scotland!' Then trumpets herald the new king.
Malcolm says he won't be long before he rewards everyone who deserves reward. He renames all of his thanes, calling them earls. They are the first earls in Scotland's history. He adds that much needs to be done in this new era. All of their exiled friends must return home and justice must be done to all those killed in the name of Macbeth and his queen, who is rumoured to have committed suicide. He says they will do all of these things at the right time in the right place and in the name of God. He thanks them all and invites them to his coronation at Scone. The trumpets play and they all exit.

Essay writing tips

Use a variety of connectives

Have a look of this list of connectives. Which of these would you choose to use?

'ADDING' DISCOURSE MARKERS

- AND
- ALSO
- AS WELL AS
- MOREOVER
- TOO
- FURTHERMORE
- ADDITIONALLY

I hope you chose 'additionally', 'furthermore' and 'moreover'. Don't be afraid to use the lesser discourse markers, as they are also useful. Just avoid using those ones over and over again. I've seen essays from Key Stage 4 students that use the same discourse marker for the opening sentence of each paragraph! Needless to say, those essays didn't get great marks!

Okay, here are some more connectives for you to look at.
Select the best ones.

'SEQUENCING' DISCOURSE MARKERS
- NEXT
- FIRSTLY
- SECONDLY
- THIRDLY
- FINALLY
- MEANWHILE
- AFTER
- THEN
- SUBSEQUENTLY

This time, I hope you chose 'subsequently' and
'meanwhile'.
Here are some more connectives for you to 'grade'!

*'ILLUSTRATING / EXEMPLIFYING' DISCOURSE
MARKERS*
- FOR EXAMPLE
- SUCH AS
- FOR INSTANCE
- IN THE CASE OF
- AS REVEALED BY
- ILLUSTRATED BY

I'd probably go for 'illustrated by' or even 'as exemplified
by' (which is not in the list!). Please feel free to add your
own examples to the lists. Strong connectives impress
examiners. Don't forget it! That's why I want you to look
at some more.

'CAUSE & EFFECT' DISCOURSE MARKERS
- BECAUSE
- SO
- THEREFORE
- THUS

- CONSEQUENTLY
- HENCE

I'm going for 'consequently' this time. How about you? What about the next batch?

'COMPARING' DISCOURSE MARKERS

- SIMILARLY
- LIKEWISE
- AS WITH
- LIKE
- EQUALLY
- IN THE SAME WAY

I'd choose 'similarly' this time. Still some more to go.

'QUALIFYING' DISCOURSE MARKERS

- BUT
- HOWEVER
- WHILE
- ALTHOUGH
- UNLESS
- EXCEPT
- APART FROM
- AS LONG AS

It's 'however' for me!

'CONTRASTING' DISCOURSE MARKERS

- WHEREAS
- INSTEAD OF
- ALTERNATIVELY
- OTHERWISE
- UNLIKE
- ON THE OTHER HAND
- CONVERSELY

I'll take 'conversely' or 'alternatively' this time.

'EMPHASISING' DISCOURSE MARKERS

- ABOVE ALL

- IN PARTICULAR
- ESPECIALLY
- SIGNIFICANTLY
- INDEED
- NOTABLY

You can breathe a sigh of relief now! It's over! No more connectives. However, now I want to put our new found skills to use in our essays.

Macbeth essay ideas
Question 1: How manipulative is Lady Macbeth (3.4 lines 53-82)?

Introduction: Define manipulation: lying and cheating in order to gain an advantage
Apply: uses language to gain the upper hand and get what she wants
Terms: rhetorical question, stichomythia, metaphor

Initially, she lies to the assembled 'friends', who are more like frightened lackeys than guests able to enjoy the hospitality of the king and queen of Scotland. She states that Macbeth 'is often' prone to mental instability, when in truth this has only been brought about by killing of Banquo and subsequent guilt. She adds that if they look at him, they will 'offend' him, which is unlikely to be true as Macbeth is consumed by his vision of Banquo's ghost. Lady Macbeth is effectively manipulating the guests, by drawing their attention to the feast and insisting that they 'feed'.

Not for the first time in the play, Lady Macbeth questions Macbeth's masculinity to force him to fall in line. She uses the following rhetoric question: 'Are you a man?' to make Macbeth modify his behaviour. She is effectively trying to man-manage Macbeth, although he seems too unstable to respond in the way that she wants.

Lady Macbeth continues to belittle her husband in order to get him to bend to her will. Using stichomythia, Shakespeare portrays her interrupting Macbeth and interjecting with her own comments on his behaviour. She remarks: 'O proper stuff', using sarcasm to put her husband down, as his behaviour is far from 'proper'.

Lady Macbeth reminds him of other visions, like that of 'the air-drawn dagger' to remind him of how prone he is to 'fear'. The metaphor of 'the very painting' reminds him of how childish he is being, as she describes his sudden outbursts of emotions as 'flaws and starts'. She is being unsympathetic, as she feels a hard line may make him see sense.

Lady Macbeth returns to the idea that Macbeth is less than a man, as she describes him as 'quite unmanned in folly'. It implies that the only way he can regain his manhood is by regaining his composure.

As her tactics are not working, Lady Macbeth tries a more subtle approach, by wooing him back to his seat and reminding him of his duties as host: 'My worthy lord,/Your noble friends do lack you.' Her ability to switch between different tactics shows how manipulative she is.

She is finding that taunts about his manhood no longer work and has adapted her manipulative tactics accordingly. In some ways, she could be viewed as loyal, as she is trying to protect her husband's position. However, by doing that, she is also ensuring that she remains Queen of Scotland, so it could be self-interest that drives her on to manipulate her mentally-shaken husband.

Question 2: How flawed is Macbeth's character?

His fatal flaw of ambition fuels new flaws, as Macbeth begins to become more deceitful as the play progresses. He says: 'Had I but died' suggesting he'd rather have died instead of Duncan. The audience can see a dangerous tyrant developing in front of them. Ironically, Macbeth refers to the 'mere lees' now that Duncan's 'wine of life is drawn'. Macbeth is one of the 'lees' or dregs that are remaining now the king has been killed.

Macbeth uses the language of deceit: the passive tense, when he says to the king's sons: 'The fountain of your blood/Is stopped'. The lack of an active verb suggests that Macbeth is refusing to take responsibility for his actions.

Another fatal flaw that Macbeth has within his character is his tendency to be rash and impetuous. Even he refers to his killing of Duncan's guards as 'fury'. He refers to the act as 'violent love'. Foreshadowing what happens later, reason, personified, is 'outran'.

Macbeth's other flaw, greed, is in evidence when he refers to Duncan's 'silver skin' and 'golden blood'. It appears that Macbeth covets financial gain as well, although it appears that he wants power more than riches.

Although at the outset of the play, he is being portrayed as a courageous, loyal soldier, his reward: the title 'Thane of Cawdor' corrupts him. The title is a poisoned chalice, given Macbeth's predecessor was executed for treason and this makes the audience wonder whether Macbeth is a victim of external evil, like the witches or if he is simply driven by internal evil, like the 'dagger' scene suggests.

However, he does show signs of being violently out of control, even at the beginning. He's fighting for a good cause initially, but that changes as he becomes more and more isolated. His escape routes become blocked as more and more blood is spilt. Nevertheless, he still possesses a conscience nearer the beginning. He regrets killing Duncan almost immediately when he says: 'wake Duncan with thy knocking. I wouldst thou could'

(II.2.74). He never believes he will be able to sleep again. He recognises he is guilty of acting through 'vaulting ambition' but does it anyway(I.7.27)

We can also argue that he is not as ambitious as Lady Macbeth. Compared to her, Macbeth is weak and would not have been able to kill Duncan. She taunts him to action, saying that he is: 'Too full o' the milk of human kindness'.

To conclude though, ambition is Macbeth's main fatal flaw as is his inability to stay on the path of righteousness. Macbeth is tempted by the witches' prophesies and propelled into murderous action by his wife.

Question 3: How in control of his feelings is Macbeth in the extract: 'Is this a dagger...cold breath gives'? (Act 2 Scene 1 - lines 33-64) and throughout the play?

There is some debate about whether Macbeth sees a real dagger or not, but surely if it were real he would not start the speech with a question. His frail state of mind suggests that he is consumed by violent, evil and murderous thoughts which are controlling him. The hallucination appears to be conjured up by the witches or by some other evil force inhabiting Macbeth's brain, making him appear completely out of control.

Macbeth's ambition is the driving force for he wants to 'clutch' his dreams through the use of violence, which is symbolised by the dagger. He is moved to action by the hallucination as he takes out a real, more 'palpable' weapon when he says: 'As this which now I draw'. The short line of iambic pentameter shows he is ready to kill and is no longer weighing up the pros and cons using lengthier lines.

However, the imagined dagger appears to lead Macbeth, as he admits it 'marshall'st' him to where Duncan sleeps. The dagger is what he sees and his sense of sight clashes with his other senses here, as it does elsewhere in the play. Nevertheless, the sight of the dagger is more motivational than any other sense in Macbeth that he may still possess.

The transferred epithet of 'ravishing strides', as it is Tarquin who is ravishing rather than his strides, emphasises how captivated Macbeth is by the idea of ruling like a tyrannical Roman emperor. Macbeth is so in love with the idea of ruling that he has suppressed his senses, aside from the sight of the dagger, which urges him to kill.

According to Wilson, Macbeth 'speaks as if watching himself in a dream'. This shows Macbeth is very much out of control. He seems to be distancing himself from the crime he is about to commit.

Although Macbeth's mind seemed to have been made up by his wife in a previous scene, now alone, he seems fearful of following through on their plan.

However, the soliloquy's regular verse suggests a certain amount of stability of intent, albeit fuelled by his unfaltering evil purpose. As there are no other characters hearing his inner thoughts, we can rightly assume that he is only deceiving himself with his hallucinations. Eventually, Macbeth pushes the dagger out of his mind and replaces it with other murderous figures: Tarquin and the wolf. This suggests a modicum of self-control as he is able to pick his visions.

This soliloquy is all about Macbeth. He doesn't mention his influential wife nor his intended victim until the second from last line. He moves from the sense of sight to sound, which emphasises how terrifying and dark his plans are. However, he is refusing to take responsibility for his actions, as he sees humans as passive and a dagger offering its handle as being in control. Even the bell 'invites' him to commit murder.

The dagger is out of reach, so Macbeth cannot control it. The structure and syntax reveal how troubled he is as the questions, exclamations, qualifications and repetitions all suggest uncertainty and anxiety. Longer sentences loaded with adjectives then add intensity and create a sense of deliberation and suspense. Finally, his repetitive resolution to kill appears glib and contrived. In a sense, we feel that Macbeth is still not resolved. His mind is not completely at rest, as he losing control of his mental faculties.

Glossary

Allegory: extended metaphor, like the grim reaper representing death, e.g. Scrooge symbolizing capitalism.

Alliteration: same consonant sound repeating, e.g. 'She sells sea shells'.

Allusion: reference to another text/person/place/event.

Ascending tricolon: sentence with three parts, each increasing in power, e.g. 'ringing, drumming, shouting'.

Aside: character speaking so some characters cannot hear what is being said. Sometimes, an aside is directly to the audience. It's a dramatic technique which reveals the character's inner thoughts and feelings.

Assonance: same vowel sounds repeating, e.g. 'Oh no, won't Joe go?'

Bathos: abrupt change from sublime to ridiculous for humorous effect.

Blank verse: lines of unrhymed iambic pentameter.

Compressed time: when the narrative is fast-forwarding through the action.

Descending tricolon: sentence with three parts, each decreasing in power, e.g. 'shouting, talking, whispering'.

Denouement: tying up loose ends, the resolution.

Diction: choice of words or vocabulary.

Didactic: used to describe literature designed to inform, instruct or pass on a moral message.

Dilated time: opposite compressed time, here the narrative is in slow motion.

Direct address: second person narrative, predominantly using the personal pronoun 'you'.

Dramatic action verb: manifests itself in physical action, e.g. I punched him in the face.

Dramatic irony: audience knows something that the character is unaware of.

Ellipsis: leaving out part of the story and allowing the reader to fill in the narrative gap.

End-stopped lines: poetic lines that end with punctuation.

Epistolary: letter or correspondence-driven narrative.

Flashback/Analepsis: going back in time to the past, interrupting the chronological sequence.

Flashforward/Prolepsis: going forward in time to the future, interrupting the chronological sequence.

Foreshadowing/Adumbrating: suggestion of plot developments that will occur later in the narrative.

Gothic: another strand of Romanticism, typically with a wild setting, a sensitive heroine, an older man with a 'piercing gaze', discontinuous structure, doppelgangers, guilt and the 'unspeakable' (according to Eve Kosofsky Sedgwick).

Hamartia: character flaw, leading to that character's downfall.

Hyperbole: exaggeration for effect.

Iambic pentameter: a line of ten syllables beginning with a lighter stress alternating with a heavier stress in its perfect form, which sounds like a heartbeat. The stress falls on the even syllables, numbers: 2, 4, 6, 8 and 10, e.g. 'When now I think you can behold such sights'.

Intertextuality: links to other literary texts.

Irony: amusing or cruel reversal of expected outcome or words meaning the opposite to their literal meaning.

Manichaean imagery: images of darkness juxtaposed with images of light, usually to show the battle of good versus evil.

Metafiction/Romantic irony: self-conscious exposure of the devices used to create 'the truth' within a work of fiction.

Motif: recurring image use of language or idea that connects the narrative together and creates a theme or mood, e.g. 'green light' in *The Great Gatsby*.

Oxymoron: contradictory terms combined, e.g. deafening silence.

Pastiche: imitation of another's work.

Pathetic fallacy: a form of personification whereby inanimate objects show human attributes, e.g. 'the sea smiled benignly'. The originator of the term, John Ruskin in 1856, used 'the cruel, crawling foam', from Kingsley's *The Sands of Dee*, as an example to clarify what he meant by the 'morbid' nature of pathetic fallacy.

Personification: concrete or abstract object made human, often simply achieved by using a capital letter or a personal pronoun, e.g. 'Nature', or describing a ship as 'she'.

Pun/Double entendre: a word with a double meaning, usually employed in witty wordplay but not always.

Retrospective: account of events after they have occurred.

Romanticism: genre celebrating the power of imagination, spriritualism and nature.

Semantic/lexical field: related words about a single concept, e.g. king, queen and prince are all concerned with royalty.

Soliloquy: character thinks aloud, but is not heard by other characters (unlike in a monologue) giving the audience access to inner thoughts and feelings.

Stichomythia: when characters speak alternate single lines of verse. The effect often shows characters vying for control, with the one interrupting appearing to have the upper hand.

Style: choice of language, form and structure, and effects produced.

Synecdoche: one part of something referring to the whole, e.g. Carker's teeth represent him in *Dombey and Son*.

Syntax: the way words and sentences are placed together.

Tetracolon climax: sentence with four parts, culminating with the last part, e.g. 'I have nothing to offer but blood, toil, tears, and sweat ' (Winston Churchill).

ABOUT THE AUTHOR

R.J. Forster is a secondary school teacher of English and a private tutor, who specialises in Shakespearean and Victorian literature. He has a first-class honours degree in Literature and an MA.

23531866R00058

Printed in Poland
by Amazon Fulfillment
Poland Sp. z o.o., Wrocław